Fishers of Men

Fishers of Men

Anita Bryant
and
Bob Green

FLEMING H. REVELL COMPANY
Old Tappan, New Jersey

Library of Congress Cataloging in Publication Data

Bryant, Anita.
    Fishers of men.

    1. Witness bearing (Christianity) I. Green, Bob,
joint author. II. Title.
BV4520.B696   248'.5   73–16091
ISBN 0–8007–0612–9

TO our little fishermen:
Bobby
Gloria
Billy and
Barbara

Contents

Introduction

The book you hold in your hands represents the outcome of something the Lord began at least four years ago.

Bob and I had no idea then, of course, that someday we'd write Fishers of Men. *At that time I had just begun—really reluctantly—to write my autobiography.*

I didn't welcome the project. In fact, I fought it all the way. It happened to coincide with the most traumatic and agonizing experiences of my life—the premature birth and near death of our twins—my own physical ordeal—long weeks of prayerful waiting before we knew our babies would survive—and long after that, fear of possible brain damage to them.

But that book I at first so dreaded to write—Mine Eyes Have Seen the Glory—was to change the course of our family's Christian experience. Written in deep thanksgiving to God, as my own simple testimony as to His goodness and

mercy in our lives, that book taught me something pro-
foundly important.

It became the first step by which I came to understand
the power of Christian witness.

More and more I begin to know just how dynamic—how
life-changing—witnessing about Jesus Christ becomes. Someone has said witnessing explains the power of the early
Christian church. After all, there was at that time no written New Testament for people to read. At first the mighty
works of Jesus were spread by word of mouth, by the testimony of those whose lives He touched and healed.

The Good News traveled. And as His apostles and fol-
lowers told others of what Jesus did and who He is, something amazing happened. The actual telling about Jesus
seems to be responsible for increasing the fantastic faith
these people had—faith that produced many healing miracles
—faith they wore as armor against danger, imprisonment,
torture—and even death.

I believe witnessing adds that special dimension to life so
many of today's Christians are seeking. I believe it provides
power they know they lack, and a very specific means by
which we can come daily closer to Christ.

Many of us fail to realize that—unfortunately. It's tragi-
cally easy to ignore the great commission: "Go ye into all the
world, and preach the gospel to every creature" (*Mark
16:15*).

Jesus said those words. But although I read them in my
Bible, somehow I thought He was speaking to someone else!

And then I wrote a book, little dreaming of repercussions
to come. Mine Eyes Have Seen the Glory *opened the door
to my witnessing. It led to writing a second book—Amazing*

Grace—*the following year. Twelve months later, with Bob's help, I wrote a third one*—Bless This House—*in which we shared our experiences in Christian marriage.*

Today Bob and I have been married more than thirteen years. We are partners not only in love, marriage, parenthood, and Christian fellowship, but also in business. Bob not only heads our household and manages my singing career, but he also heads Bob Green Productions, Inc., and Fishers of Men Opportunities, Inc.

Without Bob and our four children—Bobby, ten; Gloria Lynn, nine; and Billy and Barbara, our four-and-one-half-year-old twins—those three books I really didn't want to write never would have been written. And without Bob this book, the first I ever really yearned to write, never could have happened.

I thank God that His Holy Spirit used Bob Green, my beloved husband, as the human catalyst for some of the deepest spiritual adventures I have known.

Bob always urged me to witness. In fact, he virtually talked me into writing my Christian testimony. Bob has prayed and wept and cared about unsaved family and friends, has stirred me by his burden for witnessing, and by his example has inspired me to grow in Christ.

Bob, it seems, really believed Jesus meant each one of us to go into the world and preach the gospel. And when you read on in the Book of Acts, Jesus makes statements too plain for us to ignore:

But ye shall receive power, after that the Holy Ghost is come upon you: and ye shall be witnesses unto me both in Jerusalem, and in all Judaea, and in Samaria, and unto the uttermost part of the earth.   Acts 1:8

This obviously implies that if we obey Christ and take the gospel into the world in His Name, He will empower us beyond anything we can imagine.

In our household, we're beginning to see how this works!

Anita witnessed to me before we were married, in the sense that she made sure I knew about her faith. She wanted me to understand the place it has in her life, and that she could not marry someone who was not a born-again Christian.

At that time I was not a born-again Christian. Anita had been brought up in a strong, Christ-centered way, and I respected her faith even if I didn't know much about it. I thought it was a good thing. I wanted that influence on the kids we planned to have someday.

Gloria Roe, the gifted composer of sacred music, pianist, accompanist, and a close Christian sister of Anita's, led me to Christ the night before our marriage.

That was the first time in my life anyone ever directly witnessed to me. I went through school, athletics, the air force, through all sorts of associations with thousands of men in the service, and *nobody* ever sat me down and told me about the plan of salvation!

I'm sure there are millions of other people like me.

But when Gloria explained what I must do to be saved, when she went to the effort to win me for Christ, I found myself glad to make the decision.

So I entered into married life as a one-day-old Christian— all because someone cared enough to share the Lord with me. I felt happy about my salvation but was very ignorant about what it would mean in my life.

Bob thought I knew all the answers where faith is concerned. He was aware I had been saved as a child of eight, had grown up loving the Lord, and had been very active in the church. Therefore you can imagine Bob's surprise when he discovered that my attitudes toward witnessing seemed to differ from what he read in his Bible.

Bob literally expected me to "go into all the world, and preach the gospel." For me, on the other hand, witnessing meant appearing before groups. Even as a young child I found it easy to get up and sing my testimony. Later, as I did this more and more often, I gradually began to tell what Christ meant to me and tell of my love for Him.

As I learned more about the Word of God I'd add a few Scriptures with the songs. Because the standards of Christ entered into every facet of my life as I grew up, it was easy for me to sing and give my testimony for the Lord.

I felt everybody knew I was a Christian but I never pushed my faith on anybody else. I felt like it would be pushing. I did have the concern and burden to sing at such things as Youth for Christ rallies, but I can't remember ever quoting Scriptures or witnessing outside the church. To Bob's surprise, I had never led anyone to Christ.

No, I never had a face-to-face encounter with anyone concerning Jesus. I wasn't that knowledgeable, for one thing, and I thought what I did in the rallies and churches was enough. I thought my faith was a very personal kind of thing, and that I had no right to try to force somebody else to think as I did.

And then came Bob Green. He knew I could not marry someone outside my faith. Right up to the night before our marriage I wanted to back out, just scared to death to marry someone who was not yet a born-again Christian.

*Bob saw how much this mattered to me. He knew what he
wanted and marriage didn't scare him at all. He literally
pushed me down the aisle. My Christian faith neither turned
him off nor presented any obstacle to his accepting me. The
first time I mentioned it, he immediately agreed to join the
Baptist church.*

*There was no problem whatsoever, except that he really
didn't know to what he was agreeing. When Gloria presented
him with the truth—that he needed to be born again—that
was a whole new idea to Bob. But once he realized what she
was saying, he saw his need.*

Because Anita's friend cared enough to speak up for Jesus,
Anita and I were able to establish a Christian home.

This didn't happen overnight, however, despite my conversion experience. Our marriage limped along for several
years with us "unequally yoked"—me complacent and thinking I had done everything necessary to be a Christian in good
standing, Anita miserable because she had no spiritual leadership from me—when we were confronted with a major
crisis in our lives.

Anita gave birth to twins, and in the process she nearly
died. Doctors told us we'd probably lose the babies, who were
two and one-half months premature and very tiny. For the
first time in my life, I had to throw myself completely on
God's mercy. Brother Bill Chapman, our pastor, prayed with
Anita and me and asked us if we were prepared to accept
God's will for our babies—*no matter what that might be.*

Spiritually, that was my moment of truth. I came to understand what it is to really trust God, trust Him with everything you have.

Anita wept and sobbed, but I saw her faith hold strong.
A few weeks later, Dick Shack of the Agency for the Per-

forming Arts and I persuaded her to begin writing her first
book. God had spared our babies' lives, and I felt keenly
aware that my wife had a tremendous Christian testimony.

*In this book, as in the three earlier ones, Bob and I often
will refer to the Northwest Baptist Church in North Miami,
Florida, where we worship. Our church carries a tremendous
burden for lost souls. The Reverend Mr. F. William Chapman (our beloved pastor everyone calls "Brother Bill")
continually exhorts us to work and pray for the unsaved.*

*This influence definitely has colored our family life. Bob,
always sensitive to the need for Christian witness in our
sick world—and especially in show business—really reacts
to the inspiration of a soul-winning church.*

*We'll refer to Northwest Baptist's "fisherman ministry,"
too—a ministry we wish more churches would adopt. It
means you commit yourself to becoming active in the church
visitation program and to teaching others to witness for
Christ, as well as keeping alert to opportunities to share Him
at work, play, in the home—anywhere you go. They give you
a tiny fishhook to wear which designates you as a committed
"fisherman."*

*Bobby and Gloria were the first in our family to go forward
and become fishermen. They were so young to take that step
—pre-schoolers—but still old enough to understand the commitment they were making. When they marched to the altar
I felt tremendously convicted.*

*"Lord, if they can do that, surely I can too," I told Him.
I went forward behind my children.*

*God took me up on that action. I don't think I had fath-
omed what it would mean. There had been awesome experiences for me when I had witnessed to large audiences—in
Billy Graham Crusades, for example, or in singing to many*

*thousands of people at the Super Bowl—when I had known
the enormous power of the Holy Spirit moving through me.*

*But at that time I still never had experienced that face-to-
face confrontation of witnessing and concern for one individual's soul, that going all-out in the knowledge that you are
helping bring that person to Christ.*

*In short, I never had known pure, exhilarating, spilling-
over joy until that face-to-face witnessing came about. In my
second book,* Amazing Grace, *the Lord brought that total
personal change to me—the change that occurs when in
obedience to Him you witness to some one specific person
He has placed in your path.*

*But I knew none of that then. When I followed our older
son and daughter to the altar, I walked toward a far greater
commitment than I understood. I guess if I'd had any idea of
what was ahead I would have hedged, because I would have
been frightened.*

*In a way, when I committed myself to the fisherman pro-
gram the first person I witnessed to, through that decision,
was my own husband.*

*It was to be several months before Bob followed us, but
that big step he took was something he really wanted. That
Sunday Bob acted typically casual and offhand, however.
Turning to Charlie Morgan, our close friend and Bob's
brother in Christ, he merely said, "Let's go get a hook. I
don't have one."*

*Charlie and Bob walked together to the altar, Charlie re-
joicing all the way. He knew exactly what that commitment
meant in Bob's heart.*

Anita knows, too. In other books she has told how I used
to push her to testify publicly, and how she resisted. She felt

that if I wanted to speak out for Jesus I should do the talking and not just shove her out on the platform to do it for me.

There's a bit of truth in that, of course. I was copping out, and I'm still shy about speaking up for Christ. Anita used to be but she's not any more.

I admire Anita because after she witnesses to somebody she'll confide to me, "Wow, I'm amazed at the boldness the Holy Spirit has given me. I never used to be able to get on my knees with anybody, much less strangers, and witness to them!"

I feel I'll also reach that point, as I gain knowledge and grow in the love of Jesus. I know the Holy Spirit will give me that strength.

Sometimes an opportunity to witness comes along and out of pride or shyness or self-consciousness I blow the chance. Later I get very mad at myself for passing up the opportunity. You really suffer then.

I think that's the natural man in me, the phoniness of man on the outside. I believe the Holy Spirit has to help me shed all that phony outside shell that I'm into, so there's no cop-out regarding my embarrassment, or is this the right time, or anything like that.

I think Anita has reached the point where she lets the Holy Spirit do His thing. And I think the more willing you become to allow the Lord to use your mouth and your heart, the more this becomes possible.

Meanwhile, Brother Bill continues to preach about how too many Christians actually hide the gospel by keeping silent about it. This we blame on our personal weaknesses—weak faith, weak motivation, weak knowledge of the Bible.

We can't cop out that way. The Bible says we are to put on the whole armour of God (*see* Ephesians 6:11). And in

Anita's favorite verse of Scripture, Philippians 4:13, the Apostle Paul says: "I can do all things through Christ, which strengtheneth me."

Paul also says, "I am made all things to all men, that I might by all means save some" (1 Corinthians 9:22).

And this, I feel sure, gets it all together for the concerned Christian. That's why we'll be sharing, in this book, some things we've recently learned about witnessing in today's world—at home, on the job, out in public, with your husband, wife, children, and friends.

You learn what you can do and what you cannot do. You learn not to run ahead of God, and how not to turn people off. Also, you discover that witnessing is not just talking, but also has a lot to do with listening.

Charlotte Topping had given me a fishhook pin. So many people asked if they could wear the fishhook to signify their commitment, that we made arrangements with New Life Designs through our publisher to have the pin available to anyone wishing to wear it. Bob wears a ring with a fishhook on it, and also, sometimes, an ID tag, which I had inscribed with one of his favorite verses of Scripture:

AND HE SAITH UNTO THEM, FOLLOW ME, AND I WILL MAKE YOU FISHERS OF MEN. MATTHEW 4:19.

What wonderful news! Jesus expects us to become fishers of men. He wants us to start today, right where we are. He'll show us where and how to throw out our nets.

Jesus wants you and me to know the joy of landing precious new souls for Him. As Joshua said, "Choose you this day whom ye will serve . . ." (25:15).

For all those of us who serve Him, and who determine to follow Him all the way, this is the day to become fishers of men.

ANITA BRYANT GREEN

BOB GREEN

Fishers of Men

Anita and Bob

1 Praise the Lord!

Do you know that almost every chapter of the Bible speaks of praising God?

That was new to me. It was like a light was turned on. And, as Bob will testify, from the day I first discovered the dynamics of praise it was like the secret of the Bible opened up to me. And then things started happening in our lives—things so exciting I still can hardly bear to tell about them. That's why Bob and I will have to write this chapter together.

It all began with two verses of Scripture that changed my life: Romans 8:28 and 1 Thessalonians 5:18. After I claimed those Scriptures—claimed them to the letter—things really started popping.

We're to give thanks and praise to God in everything. This was the Apostle Paul's power, that he was able to count all as joy. My own special verse of Scripture—one I have claimed all my life—witnesses to Paul's Christian boldness: "I can do all things through Christ, which strengtheneth me" (Philippians 4:13).

But I really didn't know what that verse meant. I went back and read the portion that described Paul's life of service for Christ—2 Corinthians 11:23–30. When I read the incredible list of trials Paul went through—and triumphed over —it shook me. I realized I had taken my favorite Scripture out of context and had only a tiny inkling of what it really meant.

"And we know that all things work together for good to them who love God, to them who are the called according to his purpose," *it says in Romans 8:28.*

"Anita, that means all *things," I'd tell myself when life began to get out of hand. "God has a plan for your life. Thank him that this accident, or upset, or situation you don't understand is* working together for good *right now. Don't just blow your stack. Instead, praise God!"*

Bob immediately noticed the change in my outlook.

"Gee, you're so different. You're really sweet, and have such a different attitude about things," he'd tell me.

Things went fine for about a week, and then something went wrong on a booking. It was simply a misunderstanding, a lack of communication, but I discovered I had to dress in a short time and sing the national anthem without preparation. Chuck Bird, my conductor-arranger, didn't have the music with him. We had to do a strange arrangement, with no rehearsal, of course, and everybody feeling hassled and off-balance.

I really didn't want to do it. I was dying inside, just wanted to scream, but I bit my tongue and said, "Praise the Lord!"

It was a real test. I was at a complete disadvantage and normally would have been awfully upset. But I kept praising the Lord, and He kept me under control. We all got through it and it wasn't too bad.

That experience, like others which followed it, taught me to expect the unexpected. I don't mean I began to look for the negative, but rather to admit realistically that we cannot control the circumstances of our lives. We must learn to let God use them. We must learn that truly all things work together for good if. That promise holds true, but it all depends on the if: if we love the Lord, and if we are called according to His purpose.

And even as I began to learn these things—began really to practice praising God for everything—He was working out something beautiful for Bob and me, and for others we love.

It still overwhelms me. The best way to tell this story, in in order to show God's fantastic split-second timing, is to let Bob tell his part and I'll tell mine.

Anita and I had taken a certain step for the Lord. We had agreed to tithe not only our time and efforts, but also our dollars. I had struggled with this decision for years. Because of our tax structure and heavy business expenses, it seemed reasonable to count some of Anita's many public appearances for the Lord as actual monetary contributions—except that she didn't see it that way.

"We should give God His tithe first," Anita said. "We definitely should put God before Uncle Sam, our talent agency, our financial advisor, or our business staff."

"Honey, I know you feel that way," I'd tell her. "But do you know how high our expenses actually run—and how small a percentage is left over?" I knew she didn't know.

Eventually we decided to tithe. And that's when I began

learning the truth of what Ed Price, who heads the Florida Citrus Commission, often says.

"You can't outgive God," Ed told me.

This is true, no matter how your finances look on paper. Soon after we decided to tithe the Lord gave me an idea. The Holy Spirit just laid the thought on my heart and I prayed about it, then acted without telling Anita. I knew it was right, and I wanted to give her the surprise of her life.

I ordered a new bus for Anita. The kids and I would present it, in her honor, to the Northwest Baptist Church, for our choir's use. This would expand our church's bus ministry materially. We both felt a special burden for that. So I spoke to Brother Chapman and also to Brother Eddie Evans, Minister of Music, and both thought it a great idea. That summer we ordered the bus, expecting it to arrive in time for a great Christmas surprise.

But the Lord's timing turned out completely different. There were delays all over the place, and I felt real disappointed. Meanwhile, the secret leaked from person to person —necessarily—and I began to feel sure Anita would learn what was up.

Then, to make matters worse, what do you suppose Anita got into? She decided the Lord wanted her to work out a bus route on Miami Beach. She suddenly began to feel a real burden for the bus ministry. She'd phone the church and ask a million questions about busses—and I began to sweat.

Bob and I had dreamed about starting a bus route over on the beach for more than a year. There never seemed time to think about it—much less follow through—but the idea just wouldn't go away.

When I mentioned it to Brother Claude Wilson, our associate pastor, who heads the bus ministry, he encouraged me to get together a list of names.

Meanwhile, two of our church routes had to be discontinued for several good reasons. By that time I had begun to teach a class of eleven-year-old girls. The class, racially and economically mixed, included a number of girls who previously had received no Sunday-school training. These girls did not know Jesus, and it shocked me to realize just how important it is to go out into the neighborhoods and bring in the young people and old people who otherwise could not come to the Lord's house.

But it's hard to maintain a bus ministry, important as it is. It takes sacrifice on the part of volunteer drivers, those who ride the bus each Sunday to help the passengers, and those who visit riders at home during the week.

When we had to discontinue two of these important routes I lost about half of my Sunday-school class. That was a devastating blow to me, because I was just beginning to see progress with those girls.

Despite my personal disappointment, there was nothing to do but praise God. Those two busses now would be available for the beach route, I reflected. I was to get the list of riders together so the new route could begin, but we had a real tough schedule at that time. I kept putting it off.

Then a strange thing happened. Some neighborhood kids said some bad words into the telephone at our front gate, and I ran out and chased them home. The children disappeared into a house down the street.

"Father, just show me Your love and don't let me speak any words in anger," I quickly prayed before I rang the doorbell.

The young mother who answered the door was very nice,

and so were the little boys she summoned downstairs to talk to me. They apologized quite nicely, and I invited them to call on us sometime.

As I returned home I picked up Barbara, who I had left with Mrs. Irene Schneider, my neighbor, when I ran down the street. The minute I left those children's home the Lord told me to speak to Mrs. Schneider about the bus route. She had come to church with us before, and I knew she enjoyed it.

So Mrs. Schneider became the first name on the bus route list. Immediately I thought of a girl friend whose husband is Jewish, but who reads the Bible to her children. I knew Mrs. Schneider and my friend's three children would become the nucleus of our route. So as I took Barbara and started home (happy knowing we suddenly had four souls for the new bus route), the Lord spoke to me and told me to return very soon to that house I had just visited.

"You showed your love, even though it was a bad situation," He seemed to say. "And you're going to get those children on the bus route." At that moment I knew the Lord had started a flame in me and had sparked me toward concentrating on this project.

I got real excited. I saw how the Lord used that little ordinary neighborhood flap to put me in touch with this young family, that He had allowed me not to get angry but to show real Christian love, and I could now go back and invite them to Sunday school and church. The Lord had opened that door.

Immediately I telephoned Brother Claude Wilson. "I think God is up to something," I told him. "How many names do you need before you can start a route?"

"Two."

"Praise the Lord! Brother Wilson, let's name this the

Judah Route." I liked the idea of using the name of one of the twelve tribes of Israel, the one from which Jesus came.

Brother Wilson advised me to get started right away, now that I had some people interested. We agreed to make April 1 our target date. Another phone call produced a little boy and his mother who needed a church. Within the first half hour, God had located six people for the route!

A couple of days later after doing a personal appearance, I came home quite tired but dressed nicely (which I had not been that first time) and the Lord said for me to return to the house of the children I had chased home.

I really didn't feel like it. I felt weary, and wanted to take a bath and start fixing supper. "Fredda Walker's here and can watch the children. It won't take long. Go now," the Lord seemed to say.

When the Holy Spirit speaks so clearly you can only obey. I asked Bob to pray, and Fredda, and Bob's secretary, Marilyn Swartz. I felt a little nervous for some reason, as I walked down the street. I prayed that everything I said and did would be directed by the Holy Spirit.

The husband came to the door. The mother was asleep upstairs, and various friends were wandering in and out. Soon I discovered these people were into spiritualism. The father, non-Christian, said he did believe in Jesus Christ—as well as Buddha!

The more we talked and the more I quoted from the Word of God, the more pointless the entire conversation seemed to become. I felt I was not making contact. I knew I was in strange surroundings with strange spiritual forces working against me. I began to feel trapped and depressed.

Suddenly, God's love engulfed me. It was as if He had put a shield around me. I literally felt the love of God. Reassured, I turned to the man and said, "Just let me give

*you my point of view and tell you why I believe these
things."*

I began to give my personal testimony, quoting Scriptures
and testifying that I know the Word is true because it is
true in my own life. I felt new power and assurance now,
and the words came easily.

Then the mother came downstairs. She seemed strange and
was acting quite silly.

What pity I felt for her! Had I not had that shield of love
around me, I would have felt revolted. But now I simply
told them about the Judah Route and urged them to send
their children to church. To my surprise, they agreed. The
father said he'd also like their older child to go.

"Thank you for your concern," he said as I left.

"Thank You, Lord, for that experience," I prayed as I
walked home. Nothing except the Lord's direction would
have sent me into that house, ordinarily—that house filled
with apparently good but misdirected people—with sadness,
strange ideas—and perhaps even drugs.

Jesus tells us to go into all the world and preach the
gospel—and I had found it a pretty difficult thing just to go
down the street.

That night at dinner Bob had a great idea.

"Do you know what our church should do?" he asked.
"We should send busses to all the hotels on the ocean side
and provide a way to take tourists to church. There's no other
church really close, so I guess they normally might not make
the effort. If we could provide that service it would save
visitors about fifteen dollars in cab fare. Just think of the
souls you'd serve for Christ!"

"Bob, that's heaven-sent," I told him. I felt so excited,
because I thought Bob had a really great idea—something
no other area church had come up with.

When I phoned Brother Wilson that night he said, "That *really confirms something. Months ago Brother Al Betten- court and his wife, Carol, told us they had a burden for a beach route. This makes two of you.*

"Al Bettencourt will drive the bus. It's all ready to go."

It's so exciting to see the body of Christ performing together. In addition to Al and Carol, Bubba Howe and his wife, Irene, also volunteered to drive and work on the bus. They, with a young girl named Cathy Boehm, visited every route rider before the route started.

A week before Judah Route began, they attended a meet- ing of Christian Jews in South Miami Beach. During the course of the meeting our friends felt led to mention the bus route and ask if anyone there would be interested in joining it.

These people had been praying for some means of trans- portation to a Bible-preaching church. They nearly wept to learn of the Judah Route.

"Interested?" one old gentleman marveled. "We've been praying about this for weeks!"

That first Sunday there were thirty-six riders. You could see the hand of God in the whole thing. It touched my heart beyond telling. It was beyond anything I could imagine.

The beautiful part is, God all along delayed delivery of the bus Bob ordered. Bob wanted it for Christmas, which would have seemed perfect. Then he hoped it would arrive for my birthday in March—but still it was delayed.

Bob's bus arrived—incredibly enough—just before April 1 —the day the Judah Route began!

I had all those plans, but God's plan is perfect. Always.

Anita's bus became ready for delivery during the last week of March. Brother Charlie Walker, with Eddie Evans,

drove the bus down from Arkansas and put it under wraps
for a week.

It was somewhat hard to hide—a big, gleaming bus painted
red, white and blue, with the words of Matthew 4:19 painted
across the back.

Meanwhile, as Brother Bill and I worked out details of
presenting the bus that April 1, Anita feverishly worked out
details for beginning the Judah Route that same day. She
was intensely excited.

In church that morning, Brother Bill merely announced
there would be a presentation after the service. Meanwhile,
I had arranged to have Russ Busby, the photographer whose
work illustrates our books, present for the ceremony. We
merely told Anita we wanted pictures of her and Brother
Bill and our family in front of the church.

*How great that Bob had Russ arrive that day! He could
snap pictures of the Judah Route bus, I thought. So I sat in
church thinking and praying and thanking God for all that
was going on. My mind darted all over, playing with so many
thoughts.*

*It was April Fool's day, I told my Sunday-school class,
and we talked about what it means to be "a fool for Christ."
Bob and the children and I had come to church on the
Judah Route's initial run, and the joy of meeting new wor-
shipers filled me to overflowing. I kept thinking of a darling
eighty-six-year-old man named Mr. Ronald Green (no rela-
tion), who was so thrilled to have a way to come to church.
He was a completed Jew who had just been saved and bap-
tized two weeks before. He was so full of God's love that he
stood up in the bus while it was moving and sang the Lord's
Prayer a cappella—and he sang it beautifully! I thanked
God. . . .*

When Brother Bill issued the invitation, the Lord spoke to me and said, "Go forward and praise God for His blessing on the Judah Route."

I thought of the Scripture where Paul says one sows, one reaps, and to me this is the perfect picture of how God gives the increase. God had used us in the Judah Route, but we were just a small part of doing His will. His results had been so much larger than anything I could do of myself. I needed to praise Him for that.

"Russ Busby is taking pictures," the devil whispered to me. "Don't you think it would look a little obvious to the congregation, that it would look like you wanted to go forward to have your picture taken?" So I didn't go.

The invitation kept going, and I kept wanting to go forward but I didn't. I got so heavily burdened in my soul that I started weeping and couldn't stop.

Finally I just plunged out of my seat—bawling. I had to go to the altar. At that moment I didn't care what anybody thought, because I knew the Holy Spirit wanted me there.

"I just want to praise God for the Judah Route!" I wept. And on the card Brother Bill Castlen gave me, I wrote that I wanted God to make me more obedient to the calling and leading of His Holy Spirit. I was thinking of the times I had obeyed Him and the times I had not.

Had I not been obedient, the route would not have started when it did—and yet, it was not my doing, but God's doing. As I stood there, church members started filing outside. Bob came up and said, "Why don't you come with me?"

"I can't, Bob. I'm standing in line here."

"What about the picture?"

"Oh yes, I almost forgot." So I went outside and saw this bus and thought, "Gee, they're dedicating a bus to the bus ministry." I couldn't see the plaque on the bus, so I didn't *think a thing. There was Brother Eddie with the young people's choir, and they were singing "Pass It On."*

They said, "Stand over here next to Brother Bill," and I thought they were setting up the picture for Russ. Then I thought, "Gee, Brother Bill will stand up to the microphone for the dedication of that bus, so I'd better stand back." So I stepped back.

As Brother Bill stepped toward the mike, it simply didn't sink in. The Lord just put a blindfold over me. I still felt so emotional over the Judah Route that my mind just wasn't on what was happening. Also, I had been crying and knew I was going to look terrible for the picture.

As Brother Bill began to dedicate the bus I became aware everybody was looking at me. It took a moment to sink in. My mouth dropped open and started quivering, and for once I was speechless.

By the time Brother Bill explained the whole thing, I was weeping, and when I looked at Bob he just had this sheepish look on his face. I just ran over and put my head on his shoulder and put my arms around him. Everybody said, Oh-h-h! and I knew I was making a fool of myself, but I didn't care.

I can't tell you the joy! It was one of the happiest moments of my life. Bob really knew what would make me happy. It was too much for me—just too much to bear. It seemed to represent so much—God's goodness, Bob's growth, so many prayers answered—and I almost couldn't bear it.

It showed me how Bob loves me. It was so many things— rolled into one.

When I finally regained my composure and moved back to Brother Bill's side, he started praying. And I just wept the whole time. I couldn't stop crying. We took pictures, I cut the ribbon, and the whole thing. And I wept all day long for joy.

Here are portions of Brother Bill's dedication of the Fishers of Men bus. It was a surprise to Anita, and that's why he addressed Anita at the beginning of his speech.

Anita, this bus is given to us as a church by Bob Green and Anita Green and the Green family and the Fishers of Men ministry. After we have a word of prayer of dedication, this bus will be used in special ministries, like for our teen choir tour. We are also going to be using it in our Senior Saints ministry. Lots of times we have opportunities in the week to take our older people on some trips and we are grateful to the Lord for it. We are thankful to the Lord for His providing this because in reality He did.

Now, folks, we will have a prayer of dedication. So I want us to bow our heads and our hearts right now, every one of us, thanking the Lord for this and all the blessings that we have as a people, and asking God to bless the ministry of Fishers of Men. Little did we know a couple of years ago when we started with our fishhooks around here, all that God would be speaking to our hearts about being fishers of men! On the back of this bus it says, "Follow Me and I Will Make You Fishers of Men."

May we pray together: Our Father, it is in the Name of Jesus that we surround this bus with those who have been born again. We thank You for Your calling in our lives; we thank You that You have spoken into the heart of Bob Green to call him out in this ministry of Fishers of Men. We are so grateful, Lord, that You have touched their family and that You have given them all that You have, and Lord, they lay it at Your feet as trophies of Your grace and Your goodness. We thank You for this today. Father, we dedicate these wheels—the bus—and we ask that in the Name of Jesus You use it to bring glory to His Name wherever it is driven. May those that will be upon it be those that will share the gospel. We pray for our teen choir as they are making preparation to go this summer in all these cities and churches to sing about the Lord Jesus. We are thankful that it is a bus that will share Jesus Christ in word and song. And now, Lord, we ask You that You would take the ministry of Fishers of Men and this bus today, as we dedicate them both to You, to bring glory to the Name of Jesus who loves and saves sinners. In Jesus' Name we pray. Amen.

I can't recall any other time we surprised Anita any better. The kids enjoyed it too because they were part of it. They tithe, too, you know.

A plaque inside the bus reads:

ON APRIL 1, 1973, THIS BUS WAS DEDICATED TO THE GLORY OF GOD. IT IS TO BE USED IN THE MINISTRY OF THE LOCAL CHURCH . . . THE NORTHWEST BAPTIST CHURCH, NORTH MIAMI, FLORIDA, FOR THE PURPOSE OF PROCLAIMING JESUS CHRIST IN WORD AND SONG.   F. WILLIAM CHAPMAN, PASTOR.

These words were lettered outside the bus:

PRESENTED TO THE NORTHWEST BAPTIST CHURCH ON APRIL 1, 1973, IN HONOR OF ANITA BRYANT GREEN BY HER HUSBAND, BOB, AND CHILDREN, BARBARA, BILLY, GLORIA AND BOBBY.

Bob gave me a perfect gift. I shall never forget that day— not anything about it.

It was a day for becoming a fool for Christ. It was a day of new beginnings, a day for tears and joy and laughter. It was the day God began our Judah Route.

Only much later did I come to know what the word Judah *means.*

Would you be surprised to know that Judah *means* praise?

Anita

2 Tensions and Triumphs

One of the best ideas Bob Green and Charlie Morgan ever produced was also, in my opinion, one of the very worst! Now, all this happened last summer, when I wasn't praising God in everything.

It seemed such a great project—obviously an answer to prayer—but timed disastrously wrong.

The Anita Bryant Summer Camp for Girls, they had decided to call it. Whether it was Bob Green's brain child or that of Charlie Morgan I don't recall, but I do remember how hard I tried to squelch it.

Bob and Charlie envisioned a camp for talented girls aged eight to sixteen. It would bring together youngsters from all walks of life and different faiths, girls united by talent, whose parents aspired for their encouragement along those lines. The camp would be organized on Christian principles, though not specifically a Christian-oriented program.

The camp idea surfaced in April and soon began to take

over the month of July—the time our family usually reserves
for fishing trips, rest, and togetherness. This year I badly
needed a vacation.

Those first weeks of caring for the twins without a nurse-
maid had kept me tired and jumpy. I had suffered a linger-
ing viral infection. We had just completed writing *Bless
This House*. Definitely I wanted and deserved a rest, but
evidently Bob intended to ignore the whole thing.

Thus began a series of misunderstandings which threat-
ened all our closest relationships and tinged much of the
summer with resentment.

Bob already had decided to schedule the camp, with or
without my approval. He wanted me to give the idea my
blessing, and I didn't want to do that. Bob kept telling me
I'd only give the project a minimum of my time, that actually he and Charlie and Marabel would run the camp, but I
knew better than that. With each passing day more and
more conflict on the subject built up between us.

Meanwhile, I had just finished writing a book which con-
tained some strong statements about how a wife should
submit to her husband. I had publicly declared that I must
do unto Bob as I would do unto Christ.

You can imagine how it must have pleased the devil to
see me doing everything in my power to dissuade my husband from pursuing his plans. Oh, I thought I was perfectly
right, of course. I felt sure the camp was doomed to failure,
because the men simply lacked the time to make adequate
arrangements. I argued against it every way I knew how,
and my arguments seemed totally logical to me.

Bob and I began having lots of spats on the subject. And
as the days went by, my resentment spread to our closest
friends—Charlie and Marabel Morgan. Things gradually got
so bad I was hardly speaking to any of them.

The thing is, I felt *sure* I was right. Trying to organize a full-scale summer camp in those few months was far too ambitious a project for two men who never had done such a thing in their lives before. There seemed little chance it could succeed, and every chance it might fail. I pointed this out *daily*.

The one thing that didn't dawn on me was that the idea might have been from the Lord. God knows best, however, and nothing I could say or do would budge my husband and his loyal friend. And Marabel Morgan, my dear Christian friend and sister in Christ, chose to stick by her husband's decision instead of listening to me. The fact that she was right about *that* didn't improve my feelings, either!

So off we went in separate directions, each convinced he was *right*. Meanwhile, plans for the camp burgeoned and fell flat—all of which I had predicted. The men discovered they couldn't get horses; the animals were too frisky and too far from the Bibletown campsite at Boca Raton, Florida. Then, due to high levels of water pollution, they discovered there could be no water skiing offered.

What could they substitute for these two important attractions? How could they possibly satisfy the expectations of little girls who came to camp to have fun, as well as learn?

As tension mounted, Charlie and Marabel flew to Houston, Texas, en route to the Explo '72 convention in Dallas. That weekend in Houston they visited two Spirit-filled Christian friends—Judge Wyatt H. Heard of the 190th Judicial District of Texas, and his wife, Teddy—and suddenly Charlie found himself pouring out his anxiety about the camp.

Handing Anita Bryant Camp brochures to his friends, Charlie began to describe his vision of what the camp might mean to talented girls. He really believed in the whole thing.

"We only began working on this thing last April," he told them. "Anita is not really looking forward to it, and has come up with all kinds of reasons why she thinks it won't be a success. But the problem is this—even if she were right, it's too late to turn back now."

Teddy said she could tell it was no joking matter to Charlie. Marabel just sat quietly, not saying a word, but looking absolutely ill, as Charlie described how the camp not only had no horses—but also very few girls. Bob really wanted the girls to have a spiritual experience—but nobody knew what that might entail.

Suddenly Teddy found herself making a surprising offer. "I'll tell you what, Charlie. If it's a success this year and you do it again, why don't you let me come and do my small-group thing?

"I promise you I can teach anybody anything through the small-group experience. Spiritual, emotional, or physical, I'm convinced it's the best way to teach."

They all dropped it there. Later the Heards left for Montreat, North Carolina, for a month's vacation. They had been in the mountains only four days when Charlie Morgan phoned Teddy.

"I've just talked to Bob Green and he says you've just got to come do that small-group thing," Charlie said. "What is it?"

"There's just no way I can explain it over the phone," Teddy said. "It's just one of those things you have to experience."

"Marabel told me about it and I told Bob," Charlie related, "and we'd love to have you come do your small-group bit with the girls."

Teddy realized this was no laughing matter. She sensed the conflict and resentment among us. "I'd like to help you," she began.

"Fine! Camp starts this Sunday."

"Charlie, this is Tuesday. You've got to be kidding!"

He wasn't. Urgently, Charlie implored Teddy to do two things: to tell Wyatt the situation, and to promise we'd all pray about it. Teddy walked outside where Wyatt sat on the porch with his feet propped on the railing, reading his Bible, just settling down for a relaxing vacation with Teddy and their four children. When she recounted the conversation he got up and walked away without a word.

Thirty minutes later he told Teddy to phone Charlie Morgan and say she'd help the camp. He had prayed hard about it, and the Lord told him Teddy must go to Florida—not for Bob or Charlie's sake, but for Anita Bryant's.

Meanwhile, I found myself definitely on a collision course with Bob and the Morgans. Things had gotten terrible. Then I learned that Teddy Heard was on her way to work at the camp, and I felt curiously mixed emotions.

Teddy, you see, is a fantastic Christian leader and one of the most vibrant and beautiful women I ever met. Sometimes you meet someone who really is on your wavelength, and when your friendship also is in the Lord, that makes the whole thing even more exciting. I liked and admired Teddy instantly and longed to know her better. Now she was phoning to chat with me about the camp—and I felt pretty embarrassed. I really didn't know what to say.

When I phoned Marabel, I got no sympathy there. "Yes, I know Teddy is coming. Her husband feels the Lord is leading and she should work with those little girls.

"I'll be there too, Anita. They want me to teach a course called 'Total Girl.'"

Marabel Morgan's Total Woman course has enjoyed enormous success in Miami. She has written a book by the same title, which I was awaiting to read with great eagerness. I should have been thrilled to know Marabel would scale down her excellent course—a lecture series based on principles of womanhood and reinforced by Bible teachings on the subject—to present to those young girls.

Instead, I went back and started yelling at Bob. I told him I felt like an idiot because everybody else but me seemed to know what was going on.

Bob said I was on an ego trip, and I said the whole problem is, he never tells me anything. So we swapped a few hot words, and I said something about the devil working.

"There sure is a devil working against this camp," he said, "a little devil working on me and Charlie and everybody."

That shocked me.

"I have no joy in it any more," Bob said tiredly. "I almost don't care what happens to the whole thing."

I couldn't believe my ears. I thought I had plenty of valid complaints against the camp idea, yet I seemed to be the bad guy in this whole mess. And now Bob sounded so hurt, so tired. His tone of voice was both fed up and sad, and it kind of got to me the way he said it, because it wasn't like he'd normally do.

I listened to him. Then I went upstairs and cried. I felt brokenhearted, baffled, and miserable. We had gotten to a place where Bob was spending all his time on this dumb camp and wasn't confiding in me at all. I felt left out and upset.

Later I went out on the steps and sat there—numb—and he came out and sat with me. We exchanged some words. Then I started crying and said, "The problem is, you have shut me out completely."

"Anita, in the beginning when I was so excited about it, anytime I mentioned our plans you'd get real nasty and say you didn't want to hear about the camp or have anything to do with it."

I could see why he stopped sharing with me! At that point a question intruded itself on me: Were Bob, Marabel and Charlie all in God's will about the camp—and Anita Bryant the only one outside it?

The thought almost shocked me. I went upstairs to our room and prayed about the situation. I felt so confused by now that I didn't know what to pray. I remember saying, "Above all, Lord, I don't want to be the devil—the only monkey wrench in this whole machine.

"I don't want to be part of that camp, but also I don't want to be that. I want Your will."

Then I went downstairs and phoned Marabel. I invited her to ask Teddy to be our houseguest. Then I suggested setting up a training session Teddy wanted, among a group of women who could help us with the camp. We'd have Marabel and myself; Rosemary Conner, who assisted Bob; Jody Dunton, who nursed our newborn twins until they could be released from the hospital, then later became almost a member of our family; and Connie Foley and Bobbie Evans, wives of Miami Dolphins players; Barbara O'Neill, a friend of Marabel, and, of course, Teddy.

Marabel could hardly believe her ears. What had created this change of heart in me? I didn't bother to explain.

Then Teddy arrived, so tired she could hardly hold her eyes open. She had worked on her course for days. She came to my house ready to get a good night's sleep. Instead, I took her on a tour of the house. Room by room we toured, and in every room I poured my heart out to Teddy.

Wyatt Heard was right. God did send Teddy to minister

to me, and I found myself telling her all kinds of things, describing all my frustrations and hang-ups. Here I was with a woman I hardly knew, confessing my whole life's story!

I told her so many deep things about myself and finally said, "This must be the Holy Spirit because I don't talk to anybody in the world this way. I can't afford to."

But when friends are of the Lord, of course you trust them completely. We cried and shared, and she shared with me—well, she became as vulnerable with me as I had been with her. It was a confessing to one another, and praying our hearts out. It was wild.

At last Teddy laid her hands on me and prayed for Jesus to give me a healing in all the areas of my life, past and present, where something was broken. The healing happened immediately, judging from the peace which instantly flowed over me. It was as though Teddy's touch mended some of the jagged tears in my life.

We met with the other girls the next day, and that was just what I needed. We shared, prayed, and exchanged hopes for what the camp could accomplish. Afterwards everything—the bad relationship with Bob and all the rest of it—was healed. I no longer had the same attitude. My anger and resentment vanished.

That morning we committed ourselves to the work of the Holy Spirit, to an approach of love, and we committed to Jesus each little girl who would attend our camp.

After that, everything mushroomed. We all began to get very, very excited.

There are no words to describe what God did during the three weeks at the Anita Bryant Summer Camp for Girls. It seemed almost like a modern-day Book of Acts, at times.

Each of us worked far beyond our normal physical endurance. As I had predicted, we were far, far too under-staffed. Mail had to be picked up and answered, phones answered, questionnaires had to be filled out, laundry done.

Had it not been a Christian camp run by Christians the whole thing would have become chaotic. Instead, something amazing happened. The Holy Spirit simply invaded the hearts of each of us who had committed ourselves, and we became infused not only with adequate energy and wisdom for the tasks, but actually melded into the most creative staff imaginable.

Miracles happened from the outset. For one thing, those of us who had been squabbling all summer suddenly saw our unique talents being put daily to the test. Bob's calmness and organizational ability got some workout.

Charlie's vision and persistence had plenty of scope in this situation. Marabel's gentle, loving nature led her to give abundantly in a personal way as little girls came to share Jesus with her.

And I encouraged and exhorted the girls with their talent and appearance, of course.

And Teddy? Through the inspiration of the Holy Spirit of God, her abilities with small groups galvanized and solidified the entire camp program. Later in this book we will share some of Teddy's techniques for witnessing in this way.

As if this were not enough, God continued to add resources to our all-too-human efforts. There were the Agape Singers, a touring group of talented people headquartered in Bibletown for the summer (under the leadership of Rocky and Alice Adkins), who not only supplied know-how and elbow grease, but effectively served as counselors and Christian friends to our girls. Many people volunteered their help: Kathie Epstein, then our secretary, who has since

gone on to Oral Roberts University and joined the World
Action Singers, and her beautiful and talented young sister
Michele who was active in baton twirling and tennis. There
were also people like Rosemary Conner, my cousin Renny
Berry, Dr. Torrey Johnson, president of Bibletown, Don
Newman, music director of Bibletown and his wife, Doris,
who along with Steve Boalt taught music, and many others
who gave of their time to share in the camp.

Meanwhile, the Lord sent tremendous Christians to the
camp to spark the entire program. Colonel James Irwin, the
former astronaut who today serves Christ full time, thrilled
our campers by appearing and giving his Christian testimony.

Vonda Van Dyke, a Christian who formerly was Miss
America, sang, witnessed, and charmed our girls completely.
Kurt Kaiser, one of America's foremost Christian composers,
appeared one evening as did Dr. David Olmstead. Another
time we featured Chuck Bird, my very able conductor-
arranger and his sons Randy and Jerry Bird, who showed us
how music is printed. Joe Del Russo, my make-up man,
taught a make-up course, and my hairdresser, Donisia Ken-
nedy, and her husband, John, taught hair-styling.

And as these interesting and glamorous personalities
arrived and captivated their young audiences, they also
shared the love of Christ with these impressionable youngsters.

Day by day we watched small miracles happen. Plain
girls began to blossom. Shy girls learned to enter in. Awk-
ward ones began to feel at ease. And then—greatest gift of
all—we watched as one by one, without exception, each of
our girls learned to express love to others.

From the first day of camp until the last, one girl after

another came forward and publicly confessed Jesus as her personal Saviour. We had hoped to instill the love of Christ into our young charges, but nobody dreamed a revival would take place!

We lost count of how many girls were saved. Many Jewish girls also accepted Jesus, and we watched astonished as they told their parents about Him. To our surprise, only one mother became upset about her daughter's conversion experience.

We could write a book about the things God did in one three-week-long summer camp for young girls. As we watched girls decide to trust Jesus, as we heard their young voices lifted in song, or laughter, or Christian witness, each of us came to marvel at God's abundant plan for that "unplanned" camp.

From the first day, I realized that we all are part of the body of Christ. None dares to fall away from God's purpose, or even be lukewarm.

I shudder to think that had I not become right in my heart, had my spirit not joined with the spirits of all the others involved, I could have weakened and endangered the whole thing.

The Anita Bryant Summer Camp for Girls taught me far more than it taught any of the campers. Day in and day out I learned again and again about the power of witnessing, as we lived among the love this generates.

On the second day of our camp program, however, something dreadful happened. One of our girls suffered a painful and potentially disfiguring accident.

To everyone's amazement, God was to use this incipient tragedy as a completely triumphant testimony to His grace and love.

3   Anneliese's Miracle

It was early in the first week of camp, but Teddy Heard felt exhausted. She, like the rest of the staff, had been working eighteen-hour days. Now she hurried to her apartment, determined to seize thirty minutes of rest before dinner.

Teddy undressed, put on her nightgown, and slipped into bed. As soon as she settled in, the moment she relaxed, a thought popped into her head with astonishing clarity: *Get up and get dressed immediately, and get back over to the camp!*

She did not get up. Then the thought returned, even more forcefully this time. "I just don't believe this!" Teddy said to herself. "Don't tell me I've got to get dressed and go back over there!"

Quickly she dressed and left the apartment. A few moments later as she walked onto the campgrounds she instantly realized something terrible had happened. People were running as though a bomb had exploded. Teddy grabbed the nearest passerby and asked what was wrong.

"There has been a terrible accident," she was told. "One of the girls was diving and hit the board face first, knocking out two front teeth. Steve Boalt, one of the Bibletown staff, happened to be in the pool. He immediately brought her to the surface. Otherwise she might have drowned."

"When did it happen?" Teddy asked.

"About eight minutes ago."

Teddy realized it must have happened just as she received her first urgent message to return to the camp. She rushed to the pool. She discovered a group of some fifteen little girls who had been in the pool when the accident happened. Now they huddled together, some hysterical. They had watched as their friend was pulled out of the water, blood gushing from her mouth, and had seen her rushed away to the hospital.

"Who is it?" Teddy asked.

"Anneliese Kerr."

Anneliese—one of the most beautiful and talented girls in camp. Now two of the counselors dived repeatedly, trying to find the two lost teeth. Teddy urged them to keep diving, keep looking, and promised to rush the teeth to the hospital for reimplantation. Maybe it would work.

After repeated attempts to find the teeth, Jerry Winkler, one of the Agape Singers and a lifeguard, climbed wearily out of the pool. "It's no use," he said. "We've searched ever since it happened. I'm afraid those teeth have been sucked down the drain. They probably were right beneath the diving board, and the suction there is terrific."

Teddy said she had one of those fantastic feelings of faith just at that moment. She felt as though someone were instructing her. "Ask Jesus to find those teeth. He is interested in that child's mouth."

She looked around at the little knot of campers, some of them terrified and weeping. Then Teddy turned to Jerry and said, with real authority in her voice, "You must keep diving."

She turned to the girls. "Girls, join hands and form a circle. Let's ask Jesus Christ to find those teeth.

"We were talking just this morning about the fact that He *is* interested in our every need. He would like to show us that He will help."

Teddy said she knew they would be found. She didn't even consider that she was stepping out on faith. Brenda Evans, the counselor, responded immediately. She got the girls into a circle and they began to pray.

Then Wanda Bursztynski, one of the campers, broke away and went into the pool to dive with Jerry. As Brenda prayed, immediately Jerry came up—holding a tooth. It was perfect, without a scratch on it, and Teddy instantly saw that even the roots were intact.

They were terribly excited to have found it. The little girls started dancing up and down with joy.

Jerry and Wanda joyously resumed their search for the second tooth. For another ten minutes they dived, while Teddy waited. At last, Jerry came up and gave his companion a pitiful look.

"Well, I guess that one did go down the drain," he muttered. "But aren't we lucky to have found one?"

Then Teddy said she knew they must continue to try. "The Lord has showed us once, and He'll do it again," she told them. "All we need to do is ask Him."

"Girls, put your hands back in that circle. Jerry, go down and find that tooth."

The little girls scampered to join hands. As they did so Jerry and the camper made another dive—and just as the

prayer circle formed, Wanda came up with the second
tooth! It was as though the moment they came into prayerful union, God rewarded them.

Later that evening the little girl accepted Jesus Christ as
her personal saviour. "I want you to know now that I know
there is a God who answers prayer. I never really believed
that before, but today I was part of the answer of that
prayer."

So, for the salvation of a soul, that tooth was found. And
all those fifteen or so little girls were a part of that. Inci-
dentally, the second tooth also was in perfect condition.

Teddy rushed those precious teeth to the hospital. She
left everyone in camp in prayer for their injured friend. Nobody yet knew Anneliese's condition. Had she suffered se-
vere head injuries? Teddy approached the emergency room
with considerable trepidation.

Just as she arrived, Anneliese walked out. They had just
completed her examination and, except for the missing
teeth, she was fine. She walked up to Teddy and said, im-
ploringly, "Oh, Teddy, they're not going to make me go
home, are they?"

Teddy and Steve Boalt, grateful beyond belief, rushed
Anneliese to the dentist. Within an hour he had cleaned
and reimplanted the teeth. Meanwhile, Bob had reached
the girl's parents at their vacation home, and they soon
would arrive to take their daughter home.

As we waited for Mr. and Mrs. Richard L. Kerr's arrival,
the girls kept coming in with little love notes and words of
comfort for Anneliese, who seemed to pep up considerably
under all the attention.

Moments after her mother arrived, Mrs. Kerr noticed
something about Anneliese. "Our daughter is very quiet and

shy. We wanted her to come to this camp to learn to become more outgoing.

"And now we see her here, friendly and happy, surrounded by loving concern."

Anneliese asked to stay, and her parents extended her camp visit by another week. Her story was told each Saturday night as a testimony to the love of Jesus.

Subsequently Anneliese's story has come back to us many times. It has spread throughout Florida as an especially touching story about direct answer to specific prayer.

There's an interesting postscript to this story. Anneliese has a twin brother, Michael, who attended a camp 150 miles away from hers. The afternoon of his sister's accident Michael reported to his counselor that he felt bad. He became pale and agitated, wouldn't eat, and insisted he wanted to go home.

Nobody could understand this sudden malaise. After a few hours, Michael abruptly changed. He no longer wanted to return home, he felt cheerful, and asked for food.

Later his parents realized Michael's unexplainable mood struck just at the time of Anneliese's accident, and that Michael's return to good spirts coincided with the hour they reached Anneliese and learned she was all right.

"We never had considered the twins especially close," Mrs. Kerr said. "However, this strange experience seems to indicate that there is some sort of unusual bond between them."

As for Anneliese, she went on to become one of our most popular campers. She excelled at piano playing, but even better than that, perhaps, she won the title of "Best All 'Round Camper."

Will the tooth implants "take"? Doctors say they can't

tell for a year or two. Meanwhile, Anneliese's father expressed complete satisfaction with the way her mouth looks.
Anneliese herself points out that God would hardly go to
that much trouble on her behalf, then fail to protect the
implants.

"If I can trust Jesus to find two teeth in a swimming pool,"
she reasoned, "I guess He'll take care of them now that they
are back in my mouth.

"This accident has helped me witness about Jesus," she
said. "I never was scared and never did cry. Instead, it
brought many people close to me. It showed me how good
people can be."

4 Witnessing at Home

The hardest place in the world to maintain a good Christian witness, I'm convinced, is at home. After all, everybody there knows you!

But if we're going to talk about winning souls for Christ —and becoming a fisher of men—the most urgent starting place, obviously, is at home.

The Bible says a man is supposed to be the priest in his home (Revelation 1:6). As the head of his household, a man takes full responsibility for the spiritual training and practices his home does or does not supply.

How does that grab you? The Bible says, for example, "Train up a child in the way he should go: and when he is old, he will not depart from it" (Proverbs 22:6).

That says to me that the father, as head of his house, must train up his child through the proper and consistent use of God's Word. His daily reference to that Word and his con-

tinual study of the Bible makes one of the strongest witnesses any child ever can see.

The Bible also says, "Husbands, love your wives . . ."
(Ephesians 5:25). And in that same chapter, "Wives, submit yourselves unto your own husbands, as unto the Lord
(5:22).

What kind of witnessing is going on in your home?

Now when we speak of becoming fishermen—of attempt-
ing to win souls for Christ—we're talking not only about a
verbal witness but also of living out your life before others
so that they want what they see in you.

Ideally, that's the way we rear our kids. Someone has said
Christianity is caught, not taught. They don't hear what
Dad says nearly as well as they see what Dad does.

I found Billy and Bobby crying one day. They were mad
at each other, and there was no big reason. I couldn't help
them resolve the problem because it was such a silly fight
they were into, so I took them both by the hand and led
them into the music room and we all got down on our knees.

We prayed. Bobby prayed that Billy would forgive him
and Billy did the same thing, and when we got up after
praying they smiled and kissed each other and shook hands.

I asked four-year-old Billy why he was so happy. He said
he had forgiven Bobby in his prayers, that we are all bad,
that nobody is perfect, but he was happy because Jesus is
in his heart.

When two people are fighting and can't resolve something
it's good to stop everything and pray about it. When they
get up off their knees you see a big change in attitude.

It's hard to maintain your witness. I don't always do too
well around here—with the household staff, for example, or
my secretary. I lose my temper or say thoughtless things.

But I'm aware of this, and am much better than I used to be.

Awareness is a step in the right direction, and the Holy Spirit has to keep you there—has to keep you caring that you express the love of God instead of your own human nature. As Paul wrote in Galatians 5:22, 23, "But the fruit of the Spirit is love, joy, peace, longsuffering, gentleness, goodness, faith, meekness, temperance . . . ."

Only the Holy Spirit of God could possibly produce such fruits within the atmosphere of the typical American home! We need God daily. When our children find us praying or consulting the authority of God's Word, that is the best way a father can testify.

Does your family pray together? Anita and I can say from experience that nothing else so effectively creates a right atmosphere within a home. In our books, we frankly describe the sort of flaps sometimes produced by our nasty tempers and human failings.

Almost always, you notice, something is said about going to the family prayer altar at such a time. We installed the altar in the master bedroom of our home. Anita and I may visit the altar at any point during the day when we need to retire and pray for ourselves or someone else.

By now each of the kids has formed the same habit. And each evening the entire family closes the day with community prayers. At this time we become something a little different than parent and child, because of course we're all children in the sight of God.

At our altar as we pray aloud, confessing our sins and telling God of our concerns, we unconsciously witness one to another. As Gloria prays night after night for various little friends to come to know Jesus we become impressed with our child's burden for lost souls.

Bobby often prays for God to help him improve his school work—a good witness, for it shows us that our already-good student wants to be even better. As he speaks to the Lord about this, he's setting his parents a good example.

I have a burden for Christian families where the kids are Christian, the homes are good, and the parents are Christians—and still parents and children are not communicating.

I don't think it's enough that parents and children are Christians! I think the parents have to be aware of what's going on in their children's lives, be active and participate in the children's activities outside of the church.

Some parents spend more time on church work than in ministering to their children. People who devote themselves 100 percent to their church and yet do not provide an all-around life for their children—sports, secular activities, music, friends—provide a negative witness to their kids.

Many parents seem to stay completely unaware of what their child's interests are, outside of church. The kids cannot communicate with them at all—and that's a sin.

Some parents spend no time at all with their children. In many homes parents and children don't even eat together. Family members don't know what is going on with one another. By the time kids are teen-agers and the parents are realizing they don't know their children, they're gone.

Is yours a Christ-centered family? And if so, is your family in fellowship not only with Him, but one another?

If not, I'd suggest the parents try to think how they could become active with their kids—what activities they could naturally join. Not just church activities, but non-church things—the school basketball game, and so on.

Where can you go with your son or daughter and participate in something you'll both enjoy?

Jesus specifically commanded us to go into the world, but some parents try to create a sterile Christian environment for their children and fear for them to get outside it. If we raise our children by the power and authority of God's Word, however, we have the assurance that they can go out into the world and be well-rounded people.

The child who lives by the gospel is a spiritually tough kid, strong and unassailable. His faith protects him out in the world. This is one thing a father, by his own example, surely can teach his children.

Even if we parents manage to create an impeccable Christian home for our children, they can't stay there forever. Besides, the outreach is not there. It's just as important for Christians to witness and socialize with non-Christians as it is for Christians to fellowship with Christians.

The Lord wants us to multiply—and that does not mean just by having children. He wants us to reproduce our kind through spreading His gospel. The only way you can do that is by associating also with non-Christians.

Again, this is a way for a father to witness to his child. When a youngster sees parents who care for the salvation of those who don't know Jesus, their example teaches their child to care about others. And this world needs more caring people.

Parents, how often do you allow your children to witness to you? They have something to tell you because they know the Lord in a whole different way from you—because they're of a different generation.

They need to apply the Lord to worldly events—to different things they do. When they are confronted with college, military service, and such challenges they are going to need to know how to call on the Lord—on the athletic field, roller rink, or wherever they are.

Do you often share with your children what the Lord is doing in your life? Do you pray with them about specific problems and victories in their life? When is the last time you and your child shared the Lord with one another in any real way? Were you surprised by the spiritual maturity of your child?

Sometimes Anita and I are flabbergasted at the spiritual understanding to which one or another of our youngsters has arrived. If we didn't pray and share together, we'd have no way of knowing about it. Which brings us to the point, of course, of admitting that we parents need to *hear* our children's Christian witness. We need their fresh, hopeful, noncynical faith.

And only as a parent will share Jesus with his child can he know his child is capable of facing reality. They've got to know there's a hard, often-cruel world out there. They've got to know how to deal with the devil.

Does your family communicate well? That's a real challenge. Communication within Christian families sometimes seems even less effective than in non-Christian homes—and that shouldn't be. Christians should not take one another for granted.

Anita and I realize our children enjoy going to church, but they wouldn't enjoy it every night. There are other things they need to learn and they need to get out in all sorts of areas of life. And we need to encourage this, for Jesus' sake.

The truth is, some of us so-called Christian parents hide the gospel at home as well as everywhere else. The gospel pertains to real-life events.

Maybe parents get a holier-than-thou attitude toward what they tell the kids about the gospel. The good thing about Bobby and Gloria, Billy and Barbara, is that when they pray they know how to relate it to everyday life. They know how to apply the gospel to their own little situations, which is what the Lord intended.

And that brings me to another important parent-child form of witness. Through our behavior we can convince our kids that the Bible is as up-to-date today as it was when Jesus walked on this earth.

How do we do this? First, we consult it often. We show children by example that God has placed in His Word the answer to every problem and puzzle and question of life. We show our kids how to use a concordance. When ethical or other questions arise, we go to the Bible for the answers. The children love The Living Bible.

Prayer. Bible reading. If you are doing these things and enjoying them, if your youngsters see you growing and spiritually edified, you are providing the kind of witness Jesus intended. They are seeing the fruits of the Spirit manifested, and they are seeing that Christianity works.

It's not easy—ever. But any of us, by the grace of God, can establish a Christian home that becomes as a city set on a hill, which cannot be hid. Such a home becomes a tremendous testimony to the love and mercy of God, and glorifies Him in ways too numerous to mention.

As Paul writes in Ephesians 4:31, 32:

Let all bitterness, and wrath, and anger, and clamour, and evil speaking, be put away from you, with all malice.

And be ye kind one to another, tenderhearted, forgiving one another, even as God for Christ's sake hath forgiven you.

If any family can abide by that, they've got it made. And, with Christ's help, your family can do just that.

I like what Billy Graham told his wife, Ruth. He instructed her that their children are her ministry, and that in God's eyes her ministry well might outweigh the importance of his own.

That gives you something to think about. At any rate, most of us would agree that the most important influence we ever can have on another human soul counts for very little if we cannot influence our sons and daughters for Jesus.

This begins the day they are born, really.

What sort of witness to Christ will you give your child today?

5 God's Timetable

Doctors had detected a spot on Dad's lung. Immediate surgery had been scheduled, and the outlook seemed to indicate cancer. You can visualize our concern.

To make matters worse, I knew Dad had not accepted Jesus Christ as his Lord and Saviour. As you can imagine, I felt a terrific burden for him and knew I must witness to him at once.

I had no illusions about its being an easy job. The most difficult people to lead to the Lord, everybody says, are those who are close to you. They know all your failings.

Also, the hardest people to lead to the Lord are the really good people—the morally good ones. Somebody who is destitute and down and rotten can be reached far more easily. Someone who is seemingly happy, content, and part of a good marriage can be something else again.

And that's the problem with my parents.

Charlie Morgan and I decided to witness to Dad and ask

him to trust Jesus. We went to see him before surgery, thinking that would be an ideal time.

This was nothing new, really. Charlie and I had tried witnessing to my father before, but he never was interested. He always rejected it. Somehow, though, we thought this time might be different. Before we got to the hospital, Charlie and I prayed in the car. We asked God to help us touch Dad's heart and reach him for Jesus Christ.

The visit had been quite carefully planned. We took a slide projector along and began by showing him some slides from our Israel trip. We talked mostly about historic things, not wanting to get too religious, but keep it all very interesting to him and yet be able to move logically into the topics we hoped to talk about.

Dad seemed awfully glad to see us. His face brightened and he welcomed us enthusiastically. And he liked the slides. He listened intently as we shared our Israel experiences with him, and he asked several questions.

And then Dad reached the point we had encountered so many times before. He simply refused to go any further in the discussion. Quietly and politely, he clammed up.

We were expecting that, of course, so Charlie and I decided to be just a little more stubborn than Dad. We kept on going. I spoke, and Charlie spoke—but we got no real response.

By now I was soaked with perspiration. We were getting nowhere. Once again, Charlie and I were seemingly up against a stone wall where Dad was concerned. Now, thinking of the serious surgery ahead for him, I broke out in a cold sweat. More than anything else in the world, I longed for my father's salvation.

The hands of the clock moved forward, the doors to the

operating room were not far beyond my father's room. There was no time to waste.

"Dad, will you accept Christ as your personal Saviour?" I asked, hoping with all my heart that this time the answer would be *yes*.

He answered with complete silence.

"Okay, Dad," I responded. "How about praying with us? Please, Dad, I beg you. Please pray with us."

The look on my father's face showed me how hard it was for him to harden himself to my pleading. I felt real compassion for him as I realized he was refusing his only son something for which I was begging—literally begging.

I could imagine the conflict within Dad, even as I felt desperation within myself. I began to weep helplessly. I could only kneel beside my father's bed and reach toward him, and weep.

Dad also wept. He could not bear to see my distress; he really could not bear to refuse what I asked. Nevertheless, he did. He simply turned away from Charlie and me. As he lay rigid in his hospital bed, his face turned toward the wall, Charlie and I saw it was no use.

We gathered our slide equipment and quietly took leave of my father. Gently and—I hope—cheerfully, we said our good-byes.

I was just a little sad, because the time had seemed so right. If he would not receive Christ just before undergoing serious major surgery, when would there be a better time?

But you can't think that way. You have to remember that we must continue to pray for people to accept Jesus. My father is no exception.

We had done everything we could, I told myself. We had thought out a very careful approach, had brought slides, armed ourselves with prayer, and I believe we followed every leading of the Holy Spirit just as we should have done.

Still, Dad was not receptive.

At a time like that you can either get bitter and disillusioned—or you can call on your faith. As Charlie and I rode away we reminded one another of the fact that we are faithful in praying for Dad and Mom.

According to my Bible, this means his salvation will come—eventually. And if that be so, there's not one thing I can do to speed Dad up by a single jot—and I had better recognize that.

I believe we must pray, continue believing, witness through our example, and wait on the Lord.

Above all, you have to be willing to continue to try for the Lord—to say, "Thy will be done," not "My will be done."

As much as I wanted my father to be led to the Lord that day, and as much as I felt all circumstances were *go*, it turned out not to be the Lord's time plan.

As it turned out, also, the spot on Dad's lung presented no problem. Perhaps he had needless surgery. Perhaps he had a divine healing. Whatever the case may be, our cancer scare turned out to be a false alarm. Praise God!

"It's so important to be willing to sow seeds of the gospel," I told Anita. "Maybe you'll never see the seeds sprout or flourish. Maybe it looks like they're falling on stony ground.

"But you can't consider anything a failure. If you witness to somebody and they don't immediately get down on their knees and have a dramatic conversion scene—well, you're preparing the groundwork."

I have peace in my heart regarding my father's salvation. I expect him to accept Christ some day, and I pray for that daily. When I keep the faith with my God, He keeps it with me.

There are many instances of Christians who prayed for years for the salvation of a family member. Meanwhile, I would think, their day-by-day walk in the faith witnessed to their sincerity towards the Lord.

Marabel Morgan had an instance of this in her own life. Marabel had a favorite relative who never had been born again into the Christian life. She felt quite burdened for this man, but despite all her pleas he refused to budge on the question of faith.

Marabel continued to pray. She prayed for this man for ten years or more, and she continued to thank God for His dealings with this apparently unsaved person.

Wouldn't you think he'd be tremendously immune to salvation after resisting for that long?

As God so often does, however, the whole thing was almost too easy. Marabel, relaxed, never bothered to give her relative any sophisticated reasoning or erudite testimony. She simply showed the man a little item she carries in her purse—something called a "gospel nut."

This novelty is somewhat hard to describe. The gospel nut simply is two halves of a walnut shell glued together, with a varicolored ribbon which can be wound out to illustrate the talk Marabel gives. Each color of ribbon symbolizes part of her presentation: the gold strip reminds us of heaven, where there can be no sin; the black strip stands for sin, and the fact that all men need help in finding their way to heaven; the red represents the blood of Jesus Christ, the payment of our debt for sin; the white strip speaks to us of purity and the washing away of our sin by faith; the green strip is for growing things and our own growth through reading the Bible, praying to God, memorizing God's Word, obeying God's Word, trusting in God, and telling others about Him; the blue strip represents heavenly things and the knowledge that when we receive Christ into our hearts we have life, and we can have the abundant life right now.

Marabel Morgan discovered her simple, kindergarten-level gimmick designed to illustrate the plan of salvation truly touched this worldly and sophisticated man.

Anita was Marabel's prayer partner that day—the day he gave his life to Christ.

How many times had Marabel asked him to trust Jesus? She had completely lost count by now.

How many prayers had Marabel uttered for this man? Again, they were beyond counting.

Whatever the reason he came to Christ that day, however, I'm convinced it had been a step-by-step process. Had Marabel lost her sunny faithfulness—had she begun to nag or scold—had she given up in disgust and refused to pray for him any more—who knows what the outcome might have been?

How we react to the pain of seeing a loved one turn his face away from Christ—and continue over a period of years to reject Him—becomes a true test of our spiritual toughness.

Keep the faith. It's the best witness you've got going for you. Also, nowhere in my Bible do I discover any indication that God does not honor that.

I feel absolutely certain I shall see my father and mother accept Jesus Christ as their Lord. I continue to claim Acts 16:31 and I urge you to do the same. The Lord is faithful to His own.

6 "Reap in Joy"

Each year our church claims a Scripture, which each member adopts and prays about. Our present verses are Psalms 126:5, 6:

> They that sow in tears shall reap in joy.
> He that goeth forth and weepeth bearing precious seed, shall doubtless come again with rejoicing, bringing his sheaves with him.

That's what the real abundant life—the true Christian life— is all about. And of course this doesn't come until you get burdened with souls. Until then, despite my assurance of salvation, I just wasn't a happy Christian. Witnessing has turned my life around.

Witnessing makes you complete. God gave me a burden, and until I was able to sow in tears I wasn't able to reap in joy.

71

And so it was that one Sunday soon after our camp experience, I went forward to witness to our church body. The church was planning to sponsor a summer camp, and I felt an urgent need to share what the Lord had done in ours—and how many young lives had been won for Christ.

Members of the Northwest Baptist Church had prayed mightily for Bob and me. I needed to thank them for their prayers and tell them how abundantly the Lord had blessed us.

But as I shared with these good friends news of our overwhelming gifts from God (as I described what He had given us, and how He had helped us grow), I felt a strange certainty that this public statement must go even further. I must confess to the entire church that in the beginning my attitude toward the camp had been wrong.

This I did. My reason for going forward was primarily to thank God for leading so many, many little girls to Christ. I cried as I recalled the day-by-day commitments of precious youngsters who decided to trust Jesus.

But then I felt a strange urgency to humbly confess to all that at first I had not backed up my husband but had resisted him with all my might. I told of how events proved Bob right, that he was led of the Lord in establishing that camp, and how wrong my own attitude had been.

The confession just came out. I had been so wretched about the camp, and this became a purging thing.

Confessions of this type are private and often painful occasions. When I went forward that day it was not for the purpose of baring my soul—not at all—but rather in thanksgiving for community prayer, for the work of God's Holy Spirit in our camp, and to exhort our churchmen to support the church camp.

The last thing I meant to do was confess—and yet, that's

what the Holy Spirit had in mind for me to do. And when I obeyed Him, weeping painfully as I did so, He prepared my heart for what was to happen within the next several Sundays.

Brother Bill Chapman's sermons really hit hard. One morning, as I listened to his inspired preaching, the Lord showed me that I must volunteer to teach Sunday school.

"I can't do this, Lord," I argued silently. "What about the Sundays I must be out of town? And anyhow, I don't know the Bible well enough."

But then He flashed into my mind pictures of the Anita Bryant Summer Camp for Girls. The camp had changed me— radically. Now I knew firsthand that there's no joy to compare to that of giving of yourself, and leading someone to Christ. Through that experience, the Lord showed me I should be teaching and influencing young people.

That morning I felt an intense urge to go forward to the altar and commit myself to teaching a Sunday-school class. The devil kept asking why I must go forward and make my decision known.

"Must everything be public?" he seemed to say. "Can't you just speak to your Sunday-school superintendent quietly, without making a big deal out of this?"

But I felt this strong leading toward the altar, and I heeded it. "I have no idea where I'm needed, and I really have no business doing it, but the Lord led me to want to teach a Sunday-school class," I told Brother Bill.

Now, I don't necessarily like to go forward in church. Sometimes the Lord strips away your pride. This day I struggled mightily with myself—and then obeyed.

And when I reached the altar I happened to glance up toward the balcony, where I saw Mike and Nancy Kolen.

Mike plays football for the Miami Dolphins, and Bob and I love and admire this Christian couple. I caught Nancy's eye and smiled.

Afterwards, as I stood in line, Nancy came up to me.

"When you smiled at me I wanted to come forward too," she said. "But I felt too embarrassed. Do you think I could help you with your Sunday-school class?"

Could she?

"Are you kidding? I have been praying, 'Lord, what will I do when I have to be out of town on a weekend?' " I told her. "I need an assistant—a really capable helper. You'll be great!"

Once again I saw how important it is to follow the leading of the Holy Spirit. Had I not obeyed Him and gone forward to publicly commit myself to teaching, Nancy would not have followed my example.

Nancy is a very pretty, shy, sweet girl. My public statement encouraged her to make the commitment she longed to make—and while she could not bring herself to come stand at the altar that day, nevertheless her commitment is very real. It means as much to God as mine does.

Soon after that, our church presented Nancy and me with a thriving class of eighteen little eleven-year-old girls.

You'd have to know our church to understand the challenge of that class. Half of the group were black children, and some were unruly. Our church's bus ministry brought many children in from disadvantaged areas, and for this we praise God.

Some of our girls were untrained and unprepared for Sunday school, even at age eleven. They didn't use their Bibles, didn't prepare their lessons or learn their memory work, and usually left their Sunday-school quarterlies at home.

Nancy and I racked our brains for ways to stimulate these children. She devised a star chart so we could reward them for learning Bible verses, but even that didn't work very well.

We continued to plead and urge and pray. I prayed for each girl individually. Meanwhile, we were pulling against a strange sort of lethargy. Many of these children had unconcerned parents. Others had working parents, who could not bring their girls to church. And a few of our kids were almost too undisciplined even to attend Sunday school.

All this was good for me to see. I had virtually no experience in working with underprivileged children. Beyond that, I had almost no contact whatever with black people, and almost never had dealt with kids who were neglected or untrained.

The example set by others in our church inspired and inspirited Nancy and me. The bus ministry in particular became most important in our prayers. Committees of volunteers rode these busses—and these were long, tiring trips—to help and encourage those kids.

Sometimes children boarded the busses only half-dressed. Church members would tie their shoes, button their shirts, and comb their hair for them. These acts of love and welcome were so Christlike, so filled with the spirit of service. Jesus said, "Inasmuch as ye have done it unto one of the least of these my brethren, ye have done it unto me" (Matthew 25:40).

But despite all this, I gradually became discouraged. Teaching did not come all that easily to me, and I couldn't see any results whatever.

I made a practice of reading my Scriptures each night throughout the week so that by Saturday night I didn't have

to cram for the next day's lesson but just review. Otherwise
it's easy to be caught unprepared.

Nevertheless, we seemed to make little headway. I spent
so much time on disciplinary problems that my teaching
preparation often seemed wasted.

One morning I kept some of the girls after class and told
them their unruly behavior would have to stop. "You're
here to learn about Jesus Christ and how to follow Him,"
I told them. "You're not here to make a disturbance.

"You are letting Satan rule you.

"Still, you *are* learning to love Jesus, I know, and you are
coming to know Him better every day," I said. Though I
spoke very firmly to the girls, I spoke in love. Then we
prayed about the problem.

One Friday night the Kolens and Bob and I gave a get-
acquainted party at the church for the girls and their
families. We had ice cream and cake, party favors and
presents, and really went to some trouble to make the party
a success—yet not one single black child showed up.

That discouraged me. Little by little, I became depressed.
I saw the enormous needs, I loved the little girls and prayed
for them—yet it seemed to me that we had made little headway.

Then one Sunday morning something else—a magazine
story which portrayed my Christian witness with a sophisticated cynicism—almost succeeded in demoralizing me.

Ordinarily I pay little attention to such stories, but this
one got under my skin. I had been interviewed by an agnos-
tic and had witnessed to him sincerely, but his abridged
interview deliberately aimed at making me sound bad—and
Bob even worse. This (added to my discouragement about
the class) seemed almost like the last straw.

I went to Sunday school that morning determined to offer

my resignation to the superintendent. I had come to feel I was unfit for teaching.

That morning my dear friend Becky Barrett, another teacher, spoke up. "I don't know how many of you read the article about Anita," she said.

"She's around us all the time and we pretty much take her for granted. But we know it's not always easy for her to maintain her Christian testimony. Let's all pray for her witness."

I started crying like a baby. Becky's surprising statement somehow just made the dam break. I felt so down that morning, yet she understood.

When I could speak I raised my hand and said, "Praise the Lord! What Becky said really touched my heart. I was ready to resign from teaching today."

And then—suddenly—the tide turned. One day three of my little black girls came bringing their Bibles—and, what's more, each had memorized large chunks of the Bible verses! After Sunday school I rushed into church to find Marabel and tell her that these girls had brought their Bibles and quarterlies and really knew their verses. She was as thrilled as I was.

Penny Plummer, one of our class, is the daughter of two pillars of the church. Penny all her life has attended church faithfully, and one day I remarked on this to her parents.

"Yes, but we've seen such a change in her," her father responded. "She memorizes her Bible verses now."

"Really? I thought Penny always learned her lesson," I said, astonished.

"No, not at all," he confessed. "She never has done this before. She has a new enthusiasm."

This thrilled my heart. That was the first I suspected that my efforts might be having some effect on the girls.

Kim Harper, another of our girls, visited our church one morning with her parents. It happened to be a Sunday that I sang—Harvest Day—and gave my testimony. I happened to mention the challenge of teaching a Sunday-school class of eleven-year-old girls.

That week Kim wrote me a letter, asking if she could become a member of our class. I telephoned her and invited her to come, and she has made the most tremendous growth in the least amount of time.

I make a tremendous emphasis on witnessing. Kim came to me one day, burdened for a little friend in school. She felt she didn't have the right words to say to her—to be the right witness. Tears streamed down her cheeks as she told me this, and that really got to me.

I just loved on her, and gave her some tracts for children. "Maybe these will help," I told her. "Just pray about it beforehand, and Jesus will help you. Sometimes you're not meant to say something the first time. God will take you slowly. It won't be painful. He'll show you."

Later I happened to be talking to Kim's parents and grandparents who were visiting the church. In chatting, I probably put my foot in my mouth when I asked where they attended church. They said they had not yet selected a church home, and that Mr. Harper often had to work on Sundays.

"Don't let that stop you. Come on Sunday nights," I begged them. "It's so hard to set a Christian example for a child these days. Kim is such a precious little member of our class, and it's important that a whole family worship together."

The next Sunday that family came forward and joined the church. At Northwest Baptist we have a tremendous follow-up program of visitation, and it's the faithfulness of those people which really counts. But maybe that one little word at that time was like the watering of the seed.

I felt such a kinship with that family. "A little child shall lead them," I thought, recalling how Bobby and Gloria had led me, and then Bob, into the fisherman ministry.

I hugged Kim and said, "My little fisherman."

I knew she had witnessed to her parents. I felt so happy for her. I hugged Mr. and Mrs. Harper, too, and they had tears in their eyes.

"You know, this will make all the difference in the world in your home, and with Kim. I know you'll be so much happier for making this decision," I told them.

All my girls have shown growth: Karen Dale, Karen Summerlin, Laura Withee, Julie Singleton, Terri Mims, Kim Harper, Jeanette Husbands, Lisa Moreno, Andrea Lee, and Penny Plummer. Jeanette Husbands shared that she fights a lot with her sister.

"I didn't fight nearly so much with my sister this week," she testified recently. "I know Jesus answers prayers."

Now that's honesty. It's real and it's beautiful, and it encourages you to give more of yourself in your class, when you see these little people trying to live for Jesus.

Eventually, however, there came a blow that seemed terribly hard to absorb. Our church discontinued its bus ministry to some of the inner-city neighborhoods. Discipline had become terribly difficult to maintain. When our church bus pulled into certain streets people hurled rocks. And inside the bus, chaos sometimes took over. There seemed a real danger that something might happen to one of our kids, or an adult volunteer—so, reluctantly and heavy-heartedly, our church pulled two busses off their accustomed routes.

Thus I lost half of my class, including the three black girls who had begun to respond so beautifully. I grieved for them. I had become burdened for their little lives as indi-

viduals, and I began to pray that God would direct them
to a new church.

After a year of teaching, I must tell you God has used it
to bless me beyond measure. It forces me to dig into the
Scriptures and study God's Word with a new zeal.

I never dreamed I could teach, but God provides. When
you do a little each day it's not so bad.

Jesus said, "Feed my sheep" (John 21:16). Many people
never know this joy. They think they have nothing with
which to feed. Meanwhile, little citizens of a lost and sin-
ridden world wait outside the gates of your church, hoping
to be asked in.

These are souls ripe for harvesting for Jesus.

Difficult? Yes, it's tough. But I want to tell you that the
problems make the blessings all the sweeter. Christ will use
any of us who are willing. His Holy Spirit will supply the
wisdom and patience you require.

If you would feed His sheep, why not consider and pray
for these strayed lambs? Every town and every city has
them. They represent an urgent and special mission field for
the consecrated Christian worker.

Meanwhile, realize that the devil will do anything to dis-
courage you from committing yourself to this cause. Among
other things, he'll help you to think of teaching as sheer
responsibility—and fail to allow you to see the joy.

If you can teach—and if you *will* teach—I urge you not
only to convey the lesson, but also the gospel. Many people
fail to realize the importance of soul-winning among these
young candidates for Christ.

Too many of us witness primarily to adults, to the exclu-
sion of children. But it was Jesus who said, "Suffer little
children and forbid them not, to come unto me: for of such
is the kingdom of heaven" (Matthew 19:14).

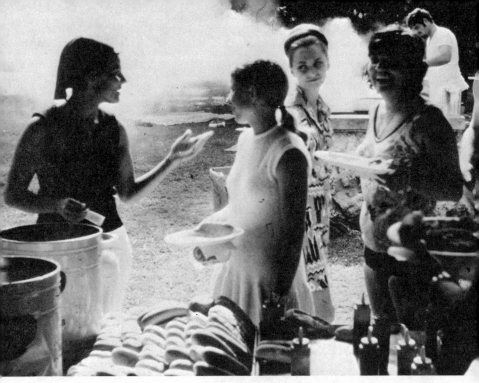

Chow time at camp as I dispense the rolls. *Below:* Skit time! Recognize the clown? It's me!

Who's the captain of this vessel? That's Bob and Bobby in the stern, while I'm sitting with Marabel Morgan to the right and Teddy Heard in the center. *Left:* A distinguished visitor comes to the Anita Bryant Summer Camp. It's Astronaut Jim Irwin surrounded by admirers.

Camp is over and it's the first day of school for the Green children: Billy, Bobby, Gloria, and Barbara. *Left:* As you know, church is a very important part of our lives. Here two-thirds of the family (Bob and I, Gloria and Bobby) take part in Sunday Worship Services with Marilyn Swartz, Bob's secretary. The twins are in the church nursery.

It's Baby Day at Northwest Baptist Church, North Miami, Florida. Northwest is a family church for Christians of all ages. *Below:* My Sunday-school class is both challenging and rewarding.

Bob and Charlie Morgan teach a class together. Here is Bob rapping with some of his students. *Below:* This is Billy Graham's prayer on the kneeling cushion I made for our family prayer altar. Charlotte Topping helped me with the background so it would be finished for Christmas. It's in needlepoint.

HOLY BIBLE

Our Father we thank Thee for all the blessings we have everyday the material things that Thou dost give us, and the spiritual things Thou dost give us. Thou hast said that except the Lord build a house, they labor in vain that build. We thank Thee that in this house Thou hast had a great part in building it; in building a marriage, building a family, building a career, and in building a home. We thank Thee for the sense of Thy Presence we feel in this home, and we pray it will always be here. We pray that this house will always glorify Jesus Christ. We thank Thee for this food and this fellowship, in Christ's name. AMEN. BILLY GRAHAM – VILLA VERDE – GOOD FRIDAY – MARCH 31, 1972

This is my favorite picture of the day the bus was dedicated. Would you ever guess from this that it was one of the happiest days of my life? I was making a fool of myself but I didn't care! *Below:* With the Judah Route bus in the background, Charlie Walker; Bob; me (I finally stopped crying!); Rev. Bill Chapman, pastor; Eddie Evans, music minister; Bill Castlen; and Claude Wilson pose on that happy April Fools' Day.

An exuberant new Christian, Mr. Ronald Green, sings on the first bus ride. *Below:* A happy moment with President and Mrs. Lyndon Johnson at the Tulsa, Oklahoma, Airport. I had just kissed Mr. President "Happy Birthday" and THEN I turned and asked his wife if it was all right! (Photo by Ben Newby, Tulsa, Oklahome).

President Johnson had requested that I sing "Mine Eyes Have Seen the Glory" at his final rites in Texas. Here the Guard of Honor folds the flag that draped the presidential casket. (Photos by Derek A. Aldridge, San Marcos, Texas.) *Below:* Former Governor of Texas John Connally and I by the grave of Lyndon Baines Johnson's mother, Rebekeh Baines Johnson, as the service draws to a close.

7   A Man's Witness

On TV news, during a sportscast, a boxer told the interviewer, "I'm a Christian. The Lord is with me, and I'm sure I'm going to win."

Have you noticed how—more and more often these days —testimonies like that turn up in print and on television? This is a witnessing age. No longer is it strange for a strong man to speak up for Jesus every chance he gets. And when you encounter an unexpected testimony that way, it makes a real impact.

Jesus said, "No man can serve two masters: for either he will hate the one, and love the other; or else he will hold to the one, and despise the other. Ye cannot serve God and mammon" (Matthew 6:24).

I'm impressed with how one of the least members of a man's body—the tongue—can turn him into a powerful servant for the Lord.

Mrs. Suzanne Stewart, an Atlanta speech pathologist who

also is a very active Christian, verifies that the tongue is
terrifically powerful. First, Suzanne recommends that you
read the third chapter of the Book of James, for God's idea
of what the tongue can do.

"To prove how physically strong your tongue is, stick it
out," she says. "Then use all the pressure of your body
against it. Amazingly enough, by exerting all your strength,
you still can't push it back in."

Try it. It's true—and this silly exercise makes you realize
your mouth might contain more power than you suspect.
Meanwhile, more and more I'm speaking out for Jesus. Very
often you hear strangers talking about religion (or lack of
it), and you just can't hold yourself back.

I heard some young college guys talking, on the tennis
courts. One guy said you can't prove that God or Jesus exist,
and I told them, "Would you believe me, if I told you I'm
not lying?"

"Yeah."

"Jesus lives in my heart," I said. "I can't prove it to you,
but I know that He lives in my heart."

It stunned him a little bit. I was either lying to him, or
I was telling him the truth. As the song says:

> He lives, He lives,
> Salvation to impart!
> You ask me how I know He lives?
> He lives within my heart.
>
> A. H. ACKLEY

The guy kind of backed off a little and said, "Yeah, I
guess that's all right for you."

A couple of years ago I probably would have let that

chance to speak pass me up. But now I just spoke right out
without thinking twice (which is a good sign!).

Someone has said a witness is supposed to do three
things: tell the truth, the whole truth, and nothing but the
truth. I don't always live up to that.

Anita and I wear these fishhooks, as you know, and also
rings with the fishhook insignia, because they make people
ask you what they are. That opens up a way to witness.
Sometimes I hate myself because I really chicken out.

On an airplane or something, maybe I get uptight if
someone asks me if I'm a big fisherman and catch great fish
and all that, and sometimes I falter.

If you're really interested in having people open up a
conversation about Jesus so you can get into witnessing and
winning souls for Christ, you have to wear something like
a fishhook. If you wear a cross in your lapel the stewardess
says, "Okay! He's wearing a cross—that means he goes to
church."

But if you're wearing a fishhook very often people will
make a remark about it, opening the way perfectly for you
to tell them about Jesus Christ. When they instigate the
discussion, this is better.

About that fishhook—people don't mind wearing a Miami
Dolphins T-shirt. Why should they mind wearing something
that says I'm proud I'm a Christian?

People say Anita and I are so lucky because we are bold
in speaking up for Christ, but she and I have our hang-ups
also. We attended the Dade County Freedom Foundation
women's tea—she and I are trustees of the Freedoms Foundation of Valley Forge—and our good friends Alice and
Wallace Hall who are also trustees invited us to help make
the award presentations.

This is a patriotic endeavor. Both of us were expected to say a few words, and we intended to offer a bunch of nice patriotic thoughts.

But one of the awards went to a school teacher—Aubrey M. Malphrus, Jr., of North Miami Senior High School—who for an acceptance speech gave his testimony for Jesus Christ. This influenced Anita so much that when it was time for her to speak she gave her testimony.

So it's well to say that even people who are well known as Christians still are influenced by other Christians who may be less well known.

We would have been guilty of hiding the gospel that day, had that young man not influenced us. Most Christians are guilty of hiding the gospel when they do not at every opportunity talk about Jesus.

One of the most fantastic testimonies I ever heard a man give happened in Houston the night Anita did a concert for the Chi Omega Alumnae Association's Chautauqua.

We had a big audience that night, and after the concert we were privileged to introduce Captain James Ray of Odessa, Texas, who had just returned home after six years of terrible experiences as a prisoner of war.

Captain Ray always had been a Christian, and before he was captured he even thought about going to the seminary. Now he shared his faith with us as he said he thought God allowed him to endure those six years *just so he could go out and witness.*

Jim Ray said one thing his captors were really afraid of was the Bible, because the men could get strength from their faith. He said they only allowed our men a Bible for one hour per year.

He told how they would trade Scriptures that they had

learned in Sunday school. That way everybody could bene-
fit from the sum total of what they remembered from the
Bible—and that's how they survived.

Now this is a man's man talking, and this is a real man's
witness. You can imagine how much this influenced me to
get even more into the Bible. You can imagine how much
the Lord can use this man's testimony, wherever he goes.

Ed Price, chairman of the Florida Citrus Commission and
a former senator, represents the kind of Christian whose
witness in deeds even outshines his words.

Anita and I really value our personal association with the
Florida citrus growers, even beyond the business relationship. When Anita appears in behalf of this organization she
enjoys the freedom to speak out for Jesus as the Holy Spirit
leads her at the time.

We're paid to entertain, and we honor that. But at the
same time, we do leave something of Christ with our audience. Many request Anita to do more sacred numbers—and
then she includes a good portion of her personal testimony.

None of this could happen, of course, without the leadership of a man like Ed Price, who lives by strong Christian
convictions. Recently Ed invited us to witness at the First
Baptist Church of Bradenton, Florida, where he's a deacon.

We had everybody back home praying for us—Charlotte
Topping, Marabel and Charlie Morgan, the whole Sunday
school—and the Lord was really powerful. I gave my testimony first, and I'm not all that used to it yet. Then Anita
spoke and sang, with Diane Graham accompanying her.

A group from the church gave a barbecue for us that
afternoon, and then we got together with the youth group.
Anita and I rapped with the kids, which really turns me on.
We discussed ways to share Christian love, ways to witness,

and all the rest. I remember challenging them to go out and win souls.

"If each person in this room were to lead one other person to Christ, and that person did the same thing, and so on, everybody in Bradenton would trust Jesus within a month," I told them.

The business of winning souls for Christ requires that a man risk himself for God. If he attempts to serve two masters, he may become very successful in the secular world, but chances are he won't have time to witness. Or he won't want his testimony to perhaps jeopardize his business dealings.

And then you meet a man like Colonel James Irwin, the astronaut who risked his life for mankind when he journeyed to the moon. Geographically, Jim Irwin has traveled farther than the rest of us ever will go.

Anita and I met Jim and Mary Irwin not long after he made that voyage. The Irwins, with astronauts Scott and Worden, and their wives, attended a reception-buffet before the Orange Bowl football game. Dan McNamara and Ernie Seiler of the Orange Bowl committee had built the halftime program around The World of Music, and Anita narrated it.

We met the Irwins that day. We had heard they are Christians and born-again believers, and we were excited to meet them. The Morgans were with us, and first thing you know, Anita was asking Marabel to do her gospel nutshell thing for the astronauts. She did a great job.

We rapped with the Irwins from the first. We invited them to Northwest Baptist to give their testimony, and promised to reciprocate at their church.

Not too long afterwards we got a phone call from them. Jim wanted us to set a date to come to Nassau Bay Church in Houston, where they worshiped. Since Anita was booked to do a convention in Houston, we worked out a date with Jim's pastor—Bill Rittenhouse.

Anita and I both gave our testimonies that morning. Then I presented Jim with a fishhook. Wow, that really seemed to touch him, and he got up and told everybody our testimony moved him so much that as he sat there, he rededicated his life to Christ.

Later Jim told us he had decided to retire from the space program and go into full-time Christian service. He filled us in on his plans for High Flight.

The project took off like a rocket. Jim got so busy traveling and speaking that he told me he only wished he could just take a year off and study the Bible. Then he had a heart attack. Doctors advised him to take a year off and do nothing.

Months later, the phone rang one day and it was Jim Irwin. The Lord had given him a fantastic idea. High Flight, at his headquarters at Colorado Springs, Colorado, was going to sponsor a series of spiritual retreats for America's returned prisoners of war and their families, plus the families of men still officially missing in action.

"They've been given the keys to their cities," Jim said. "People have given them cars and vacation trips and parades and bottles of champagne.

"But who is going to give these men and their families what they really need?"

When Jim Irwin asked Anita and me to join in this effort and give our personal testimonies to these people, we both were tremendously touched and honored. It's one of the greatest privileges we have ever enjoyed. Pastor Bill Rittenhouse, Rocky Forshey, the Irwins, Heards, and numerous other dedicated Christians blazed a new trail for the Lord. Their witness for Jesus was tremendous. They stepped out in complete faith even with a 300-thousand-dollar debt to pay, and we are confident that Christians from all over the country will want to share in this ministry.

This is heavy stuff. I'm seeing again and again how much weight one man's witness for Christ can carry. And I'm not saying you have to be an astronaut, a hero, or a representative of big business.

Jesus himself chose fishermen, a tax collector, a tent maker.

All this encourages me. One of my enterprises is called Fishers of Men Opportunities, Inc. This essentially is a Christian talent agency, aimed at providing well-known Christians to help churches over America put on revivals and other programs.

The corporation is coming along fine. Because there is no pressure towards financial gain, and because we are doing the Lord's work, it's really a joy.

People who have a talent and a Christian testimony and are looking for outlets to be of service to God—that's what our organization exists for. As long as we do things for the glory of God, we're in good shape.

The experiences and recognition we get even in the secular world, God can use. We've seen the impact a Captain Ray or a Colonel Irwin can have on the nation as they witness to the power of God.

Fishers of Men Opportunities, Inc. places these two men in churches, along with such dedicated Christians as young Kathie Epstein; baseball player Alvin Dark; Janet Lynn, the pretty champion ice skater; Jane Jayroe, Miss America of 1967; Howard Twilley, Norm Evans and Mike

Kolen of the Miami Dolphins football team; Senator Mark Hatfield, and, of course, Anita Bryant.

If Anita Bryant hadn't cut million-copy records and done all these things, sure she still would have had a Christian testimony. However, partly as a result of her secular successes, I believe she has far more impact and influence for the Lord.

By the way, the day we testified at Ed Price's church I presented him with a fishhook. Later he told me that the very next day a man asked him about it, one thing led to another, and Ed found himself leading someone to Christ!

This makes you stop and think.

How much manpower is going to waste around your house? How often do you speak up for Jesus?

Do you know the strength of your own tongue?

Behold, we put bits in the horses' mouths, that they may obey us; and we turn about their whole body.

Behold also the ships, which though they be so great, and are driven of fierce winds, yet are they turned about with a very small helm, whithersoever the governor listeth.

Even so the tongue is a little member, and boasteth great things. Behold, how great a matter a little fire kindleth!

James 3:3–5

8 Two by Two

So often our Christian growth is a two-by-two sort of thing —and especially when it comes to witnessing.

I can't remember when I discovered that we usually seem to operate in pairs: Charlie and Bob; Nancy Kolen and me; Charlotte Topping and Marabel Morgan; Marabel and me. And so on.

When I go visiting for our church, I go with Kathy Miller, who was my Sunday-school teacher. And whenever Bob or I have a special burden for someone, invariably we send out an SOS to Brother Bill.

All this is very logical when you stop to think about it. Jesus' disciples usually went out two by two. Three of them were present—Peter, James and John—even during His amazing Transfiguration.

Later, the Apostle Paul and the others seemed to travel, minister, and witness in pairs, at least.

And in Matthew 18:20, Jesus tells us: "For where two or

three are gathered together in my name, there am I in the midst of them."

I have a theory that many Christians who feel paralyzed by the idea of witnessing for the Lord are trying to do it solo. When there are two of you—one to speak, one to quietly pray—it goes better.

So far as out-and-out witnessing goes, Marabel Morgan really has been a testimony to me. Her Christian life flourished all those years ago with Campus Crusade for Christ. Since then, as a young wife and mother, Marabel has set an example in continuing to witness, and she has taught me much about the how-to of witnessing.

She has shown me many tools. She and Charlie were the first Christians to teach us about the four spiritual laws. It was Marabel who discovered the gospel nutshell, with which she demonstrates God's plan of salvation. She used one dumb little nutshell to lead seven people to Christ. I love to watch her do it. She is so gentle, and she glows when she speaks of God's love for us.

Marabel and I are not together all that much, in one sense. Practically speaking, our lives are quite separate. But we are the closest of prayer partners. For instance, at the very hour she is to give a Total Woman class, I pray for her. I am her prayer partner in everything, and she in mine. The Morgans and the Greens have a deal whereby we can phone each other at any hour of day or night for prayer.

Bob and Charlie go out together and witness to friends, often using slides and movies. They are such close friends and spiritual brothers, and their teamwork is excellent. For some time they shared teaching a Sunday-school class of college-age kids, encouraging them to share and witness for the Lord.

Renny Berry, my cousin and an ordained Baptist minister, who is now pastor of the First Baptist Church in Mulvane, Kansas, is Marabel Morgan's male counterpart in my life. Renny has become in every sense my Christian brother. When he was in Miami, oftentimes he was the one to whom I turned when I needed help in witnessing. Renny is not only a good sounding board for me, but he provides me the Scriptures I need for specific purposes. Beyond that, he boosts me constantly with his loving encouragement and his prayers. With his wife Janet, Renny Berry has become the utmost source of strength and inspiration towards my desire to win souls.

Several months ago Jody Dunton and I (she's the professional nurse who helped the Lord keep our twins alive) were on our way to the hospital to visit with Renny, who was confined there briefly.

We went out two by two that day, little dreaming that the Lord planned for us to witness. It was just a pop call on Renny, and neither of us had a Bible along.

At the elevator, a gentleman stopped us. He appeared to be quite nervous. Apologizing for approaching me, he explained that his daughter had given premature birth to her first child, a son, and the infant was near death. In an effort to comfort the young woman, someone had given her a copy of my book—*Mine Eyes Have Seen the Glory*—in which I told about our experiences with premature twins.

"Miss Bryant, could you please stop in and see my daughter for just a moment?" he asked. "It would mean so very much to her."

My heart went out to him.

"I know exactly how you all feel," I said. "Is your daughter a Christian?"

"Yes."

"A born-again Christian?"

"I . . . I think so."

Quickly I agreed to visit his daughter, after we called on
Renny. And once in Renny's room, we asked for help with
some Scriptures. Why, oh why, had we not brought Bibles
with us?

"We'd better pray about it," Renny said, and we did.

"Anita, the Lord seems to be telling me to suggest Proverbs 3:5, 6: 'Trust in the Lord with all thine heart; and lean
not unto thine own understanding. In all thy ways acknowl-
edge him, and he shall direct thy paths.'"

She was a sweet-faced little blonde, only seventeen or so,
and her husband was nearly as young. They looked heart-
broken. Their parents looked sad and exhausted.

I felt very aware of Jody's presence beside me. Obviously
I was the one who would do the talking this time but I knew
Jody would pray. So I began to share, briefly, how we had
experienced the incredible love of God in the act of giving
up our babies into His care.

"Maybe your need will bring you close to the Lord, so
that He can have His way in your life," I told them. "As
much as you want your baby—and I *know* what that is, because I've been there—it's important that you love God and
trust Him with this little life.

"God has a plan for your baby's life. You cannot see
ahead, but He can. Perhaps your child has brain damage
and He knows you're not strong enough for that and maybe
it's God's will to take him home. Or perhaps God is using
his little weak body as a means of making you desperately
dependent on Him for your baby's survival."

We continued to share this way for a while, and then I

prayed for them. I just laid a hand on each one of them and asked God to provide them with His peace that passeth all understanding. We all cried together.

I also asked Him to make them able to pray together after I left, and just give themselves and that baby and the whole situation over to God.

We didn't stay long. As we rose to leave, Jody, so very compassionately, turned to the little mother. Explaining that she was a nurse who specializes in neonatology (care of the newborn), Jody promised to look in on the baby and examine him. Suddenly the infant's grandfather looked startled.

"What did you say your name is?" he asked.

"Jody Dunton."

Looking amazed, he slowly drew a card from his pocket. *"Jody Dunton,"* he repeated, staring at the name scrawled across the card. Someone, learning that the baby had been transferred to the Premature Section at Jackson Memorial Hospital, Jody's department, had written her name and suggested that these people look her up.

We all just stared at one another. I think we all had cold chills.

"Isn't that just like the Lord to send Jody here early, to comfort this baby's mother!" I exclaimed. And then we all rejoiced.

It seemed such a fantastic coincidence, unless you understand how the Lord works. Even before we started out to visit Renny, God had a specific mission for Jody. She came along with me to help support me with her prayers—but it really was Jody, I'm convinced, that the Lord specially wanted in that room.

Meanwhile, He showed me—in the most direct, concrete

way possible—a specific example of His use of my written testimony. It made me feel strange and humble to see my book used of the Lord.

Jody and I just praised the Lord that night, feeling so filled with the sense of His love and specific direction. We had gone together to the hospital because Jody just happened to be over at the house when I started out. I went that evening because it was the only time I had free to go. And then we just happened to encounter that gentleman in the hospital lobby. He could just as well not have come down at that exact moment—or he might not have recognized me!

No, it was obvious to me that this was yet another example of God's split-second timing. Quickly I shared the experience with Marabel so she could marvel with us over the Lord's loving kindness, and so she could begin praying for the baby.

Later, at Jackson Memorial Hospital, the couple sought out Jody. About that time, the infant started improving. Soon he weighed five pounds and could go home.

Soon after that I received a beautiful card from the young couple, thanking me and assuring me that they had come close to the Lord through this experience. It was a beautiful gift to all of us.

I shared, from a distance, in an unusual conversion experience fostered by Marabel. This involved a man she met quite by accident—or, by human standards it would seem so, though I believe God planned it otherwise. It's a strange story.

One day, outside her children's school, Marabel left her lights on and her car wouldn't start. Another mother gave her a lift to where she was going, and thus she happened to ride in the car with the woman's father.

During the course of the conversation, the man (a prominent and successful gentleman) offered the observation that life really isn't worth living.

"Oh, sir! If you would give me a few moments of your time . . . maybe have lunch with me soon . . . I think I have what you're looking for," Marabel ventured. (I can imagine the stricken look on her face.)

"I bet you do!" he kidded her.

"No, you don't understand," Marabel continued earnestly. She explained that she had the answers to the spiritual needs he felt. She spoke so sweetly and convincingly that her new-found friend agreed to have lunch with her and his daughter that Friday.

That day Marabel phoned me, explained the situation, and asked for prayer during the luncheon appointment. At that moment I happened to have Jeannette Royster, a friend of Charlotte Topping, visiting me.

Jeannette and I went to the prayer altar. I prayed the Lord would prepare the man's heart so he would accept Christ, and that every word Marabel said would be of the Holy Spirit. Jeannette prayed a similar prayer and got very excited. She said she'd never before had quite that kind of adventure.

Later that afternoon, Marabel reported back to me.

"Praise the Lord, the man is saved! I really felt the power of your prayers.

"Anita, he was as ready as anything. It was like feeding baby food to a baby!"

When I called Jeannette to tell her, she actually squealed with excitement.

One of the most important Christian partnerships in my life concerns Anne Veracchi, a friend who lives in Boston.

Anne and I see each other only about once a year, but we enjoy an extremely meaningful relationship for which I am very grateful.

We first met in August, 1963, when I appeared in Framingham, Massachusetts, in *Annie Get Your Gun*. Anne, who is the most loyal fan anybody ever had, sent me roses that night. She went on from there to do all sorts of wonderful things in my behalf. And these things still happen.

Several months ago Anne appeared at the Florida Citrus Queen pageant and presented me with a plaque provided by some ninety fans. This is amazing, considering there is no organized fan club—just a mailing list Anne maintains.

In 1967, Anne Veracchi did an especially wonderful thing for me. She took over my mailing list. She feels that anyone who writes to me deserves a reply—and I agree—but we both know that's impossible, if I'm to do everything else I'm supposed to do.

Anne replies to many of my letters. I scribble a note concerning what to write, of course, but it's Anne who puts it in proper form. When I receive a prayer request I immediately pray right there at my desk. Sometimes, if a person has a special problem, I phone Brother Bill and he helps me find Scriptures to comfort them in their needs.

Anne has a real talent for answering my mail just as I would do it. She has great compassion and an instinctive rapport with people, and these letters in a real way have become a ministry for her.

As the months roll into years it touches my heart to know that Anne prays over this mail even as I do. She answers as I would, and all of this she does as unto the Lord. In a real sense, we have gone two by two for some time, and I thank God for her.

As we go forward in partnership for the Lord I look forward to having more prayer time with Bob alone, just praying and reading the Bible together—the ultimate intimacy.

I yearn to grow into that. We have it from time to time, of course, but it's not yet a habit.

Meanwhile, there are signs that we are building toward that spiritual closeness. I'm thinking of a time in Washington, D.C., where I had performed and given my testimony at a prayer breakfast for the Congressional Wives Club.

While there I met Michele Metrinko, a former Miss World. I wondered why the Lord had our paths cross again (we had been together during a Bob Hope overseas tour) and I wasn't long in finding out. Bob and I could have been witnessing to Michele and others on the Bob Hope trips, of course, but at that time we didn't witness.

Now here was Michele again, with her sisters, Marsha and Margot—three brilliant girls, all multi-lingual and beautiful. Michele today is a graduate of Harvard Law School. Margot attends Princeton, and Marsha is an actress. We met for dinner at the hotel and spent an evening talking about the Lord and giving our testimony.

We spent the whole evening with the gospel.

Usually, at a time like that, Bob lets me do all the talking. This time, however, he chimed in and told about Paul, when they were in jail and God opened the doors, and the guard started to kill himself. When Paul restrained him, the guard fell on his knees and said, "Sirs, what must I do to be saved?" (Acts 16:30).

"Believe on the Lord Jesus Christ, and thou shalt be saved . . ." Paul and Silas answered (v. 31).

I felt really excited because that was one of the first times I ever heard Bob share about someone's salvation.

Bob says he hates himself when he has something on his heart to say and then doesn't say it. Maybe I don't give him

a chance. That night, however, the Holy Spirit allowed him
to open up, and allowed me to shut up and let him tell it.

Before we left I said, "Can we all pray together?"

We held hands in a circle and prayed for each girl's need.
We asked God to help them find what they seek, and that
they would come to know the Lord.

For me, this was a real adventure in going out two by two
with my own husband. I cherished that evening, and pray
that God will give us many more like it.

Bob, of course, has been at my side for years as I witnessed
publicly. I need his support and love, depend on his prayers,
and always feel intensely close to him at such times.

Several months ago he presented—several times in a row—
a request for my witness, from the Grace Memorial United
Methodist Church in Atlanta.

I kept turning down the request. Our schedule was ridicu-
lous at that time, and I knew I could take no more. Bob,
meanwhile, was becoming increasingly unhappy about the
situation.

One night Bob phoned me from his office in another part
of the house. "I have a burden," he said. This grabbed my
attention at once, because that's not Bob's phrase.

"I have a burden on my heart. There's this Reverend Sam
Coker—the last letter he sent—I've already answered no, but
I can't get it out of my mind.

"Anita, he's a born-again Christian, a Spirit-filled man, and
I can't get over the sweetness of his letter. I feel led of the
Lord—and I've been praying about this—I feel led of the Lord
that we've just got to do it."

I felt somewhat stunned.

"Before you say no, I think I have a way to work it out,"
he continued. "We're due to be at Calvary Baptist Church
in New York City on Saturday night for the 125th anniversary

celebration. After the radio and TV rally there, we can get a flight to Atlanta which arrives around two in the morning. I've called Gloria Roe and she will be able, after playing for you Saturday night, to travel with us.

"You can get six hours' sleep, and we can do that early service and get home."

I saw he had every detail worked out.

"Do you really feel that strongly about it?" I asked.

"Yes."

"Then we'll do it."

Bob said when he phoned the Reverend Coker he almost wept on the phone. "The Lord is faithful. Praise the Lord!" he said. Bob told me it almost broke his heart.

Then the story came out. Here's a man who had written us and had prayed, and all along everybody said, "You're not going to get her." And we had declined his requests, but he remained faithful for months. He prayed all that time.

No wonder Bob felt so moved!

In New York, there were delays. A mechanical difficulty also delayed the flight to Atlanta. "Bob, it's Satan," I said. We began to worry that we couldn't make it after all. We arrived at dawn. Soon we faced a congregation that packed the large church even to the basement.

This affected me so much. I saw the power of Sam Coker's trust in the Lord. I saw also how Bob was used of the Holy Spirit. It was a revelation to me that I was the one who nearly cut it off, even though I was supposed to be such a Spirit-filled Christian!

Two by two. Bob was with me as the Lord helped me witness despite a sleepless night. There was a problem in that the testimony was to be televised over the state, it turned out, and my witness could not go over forty minutes.

I prayed God would give me the right words—the right

timing. I was bone-tired and had the beginning of a cough
and the flu bug, and I knew I couldn't pace myself. God
would have to do it. I was hoarse and had no voice.

That morning, God provided everything. He provided the
power, the voice, the words, the testimony—and all in forty
minutes. It worked out perfectly.

Two-by-two witnessing almost has become a prerequisite
for me. I'll call Marabel, or I'll call Brother Bill to ask the
church to pray.

The prayer together, the power together, the upholding
of one another, and the sharing and learning you have together becomes something phenomenal.

I love remembering that feeling of closeness to Bob I felt
when he called me back after phoning Sam Coker to tell him
we'd come to Atlanta after all.

"Honey, I've just had the most wonderful experience," he
said. "You don't know how good it made me feel to tell that
man you would do it, because I feel like he's another Brother
Bill. Thank you, Anita. I know we're doing the right thing."

That was one of those moments of understanding that
where two or three are gathered together in His name, He
truly is there in the midst of us.

9 Don't Turn Them Off

Every person is an individual and every unsaved person has to be treated as an individual, and approached differently from all others. If you don't approach these people correctly you will not only turn them off toward yourself, but also for future witnesses—and maybe even forever.

The best witness, of course, is for people to see Jesus in you.

We went to Open House at Bobby's school one night and Bobby's young teacher told us, "I go home and tell my husband how happy and content Bobby is, how unspoiled, and I just don't understand why he's so different from most children his age."

We told her it's the Lord in him. We were glad his teacher had noticed it made Bobby Green somehow different. What Bobby did was ideal because he didn't do or say a thing, yet somebody noticed something in him that they desired and admired.

Some Christians, in their zeal, really do turn people off.

If you're a salesman, and you're going to approach a certain kind of individual, and it's an important sale you're going to make, you do just a little bit of thinking about how to approach this man differently than you would somebody else.

We have learned it sometimes has quite an adverse effect on a person to hit him with the gospel prematurely. Sometimes you have to use a little psychology, not just knock on the door, put a Bible in somebody's face, and ask him if he has been saved.

On the other hand, there are plenty of Christians who look so sloppy and dowdy that I wonder why anybody in the world should want to follow their example. Nobody says a Christian should be old-fashioned and not up with the times, or anything like that, but they've really got to be a complete Christian.

That includes a good personality, attractiveness, good health, and vitality. Kathie Epstein comes to my mind. She's vibrant, wholesome, and beautiful—a beauty-pageant winner, and talented besides—yet she's completely modest. You'd never say she's at all hampered by being a Christian.

One important way for a Christian to witness is through having fun and being fun. Non-Christians sometimes think of us as stick-in-the-mud types. I think it's important for others to see Christ in you—and also to see that Christians can and do have a good time.

There's a certain wonderful Christian freedom that comes from just being yourself. We've had comments that we have so much fellowship and fun at our parties, and some non-Christians comment they're amazed at how much fun they had, and there was no liquor, no carousing.

They're surprised they could have such a good time in a Christian environment. If people could do more of this, it would help lead others to Christ.

A lot of people fear becoming Christian because they have the idea they'll have to be very rigid and sober-faced, and give up all good times. Actually, it's a witness to have a good time—and our Lord certainly did.

The Bible tells us He enjoyed companionship, and that He actually was accused of being a winebibber and a glutton!

Sometimes we witness best by what we don't say. The angry word. The profanity.

When Charlie and I play tennis or go fishing with some of the Christians on the Dolphins' team—Mike Kolen, Norm Evans, or Howard Twilley—we knock our brains out trying to beat one another at the sport but never use one bit of profanity.

We do everything the other guys out there do, but the others are out there swearing. To do without swearing doesn't hurt our game.

I think everyone should examine his churchgoing from time to time.

Do I go enough? If I'm going to church every time the doors open, why do I go? Is my ultimate goal some sort of self-satisfaction—a cop-out from other forms of life—or am I sincerely trying to win souls for Christ?

Do I go for some sort of selfish display? For something to do with my time?

Is churchgoing my only social outlet?

Also, do I go to church so much—and make sure non-Christians know about it—and then it does not prove consistent with the way I live?

Non-Christians look on religious displays and weigh them against our lives—and if it doesn't match up, they'll pick at you for it. Hypocrisy.

It all boils down to two questions: Am I trying to win

souls to Christ? And am I the kind of person who can, by my example, win souls to Him?

Many times, in being willing to be an agent for leading someone to Christ, people will get discouraged, will knock their brains out witnessing to somebody with the hopes of leading them to the Lord. If it doesn't seem to come off they'll get discouraged. Eventually the person will be led to the Lord—but by somebody else.

Often one man's salvation represents a lot of combined effort. The Lord uses many people to win one soul. You might witness to someone and see no results, yet a year later that person might go forward in church someplace and accept Jesus—possibly because the seed you planted a year ago just came up in his heart.

If we can remember that principle, we don't have to "oversell" the non-Christian until we turn him completely off.

It's like a fighter who gets knocked out. Very few fighters get knocked out from one punch. It's a series of punches that weaken and weaken him, and then one shot puts him down— but it's the cumulative effect of a series of blows that really gets him.

But if you don't bother to try to witness, you'll never make these mistakes I mention, of course. And so many Christians never bother to try.

In our church, soul-winning is the name of the game.

That's what Christianity is about. That's the whole Bible. Go out and preach the Word—that's the whole thing—and it runs all through the Bible.

Learning the *do's* and *don'ts* of witnessing reminds me of taking tennis lessons. In the beginning I hit a bad shot and didn't know why I hit a bad shot. That's Stage One.

Stage Two is hitting the bad shot, but knowing that you hit it. Stage Three will be a fairly consistent ability to hit the good shot most of the time. You have to get to that second stage—where you know what you're doing wrong—before you can correct it.

After I hit a bad stroke and miss the ball, I momentarily get angry with myself, because I know what I did wrong. You do that enough times, and eventually you get consistently good.

That's like sin. The first stage is sinning and not knowing it. The second stage is sinning, and feeling sorry. But you keep trying to reach that mark—even though you know you'll ultimately never be perfect.

In tennis, if you hit the bad stroke and start playing the game without taking lessons for a long time, that bad stroke will become habit. You may be getting it over the net pretty well, but you're hitting it incorrectly—and you're grooved into that habit. You're inserting that bad habit into your life— your game.

Do that long enough, and when time comes to take your lessons it's doubly hard to go backwards and unlearn that bad habit. That's why it's important to learn Christian principles as early as possible.

When we faulty human beings, with all our sinful natures, somehow learn to become channels for the Holy Spirit and let Him work His own thing through us, we don't have to worry about turning people off. They'll want what they see in us.

As someone said, "The Holy Spirit is a gentleman." He won't let us be coarse, excessive, or extreme.

I love watching Anita become a true channel for Him. I think my wife has the real gift of naturalness and joy in the Lord, and I always have enjoyed hearing her witness.

Teddy Heard told me about one particular episode which Anita may have forgotten. It touched my heart so much that I decided to share it with you, and I hope Anita won't mind.

I got Teddy to tell about this testimony in her own words, and I'll give it to you straight off the tape just as Teddy told it. I think it's a perfect example of how the Holy Spirit can use a yielded Christian.

"Anita, Marabel, and I were in Austin, Texas. We heard that Luci Nugent, daughter of the late President Lyndon B. Johnson, was in the hospital there. She had had an ear operation and was very ill.

"Anita wanted to go see her. It turned out Luci was so sick that only Anita could go in. President and Mrs. Johnson were in her room. Anita went in and visited for a while, then withdrew.

"Meanwhile my little aunt, ninety-two years old, was dying of cancer in another hospital in Austin. She had been in and out of a coma for about a week. I had told Anita and Marabel I really wanted to go by and see Sister, because this might be our last opportunity.

"It was getting late. Anita's show was to start about an hour and twenty minutes from the time she left Luci's bedside. I suggested that she and Marabel scoot back to the hotel and let me go on and see Sister.

"Anita just looked at me. 'You know, Teddy, God is no respecter of persons,' she said. 'Luci Nugent is no more important to God than your little ninety-two-year-old aunt.

" 'I've never met a ninety-two-year-old person who has lived her whole life for Christ. I want to go with you.'

"We went, and found just this precious little shriveled old lady. I went in by myself and held her hand and talked to her. She opened her eyes and smiled, and I really felt she knew it was me.

"I was very moved. It hit me what Anita had said, that she really had lived her life for the Lord, and now here she was dying without any pain at all. I felt very sustained in prayer.

"About that time, Anita came into the room. I had tears streaming down my face, thinking about Sister and what she had meant in my life—what an influence she had been.

"Anita went over and took her hand, and leaned over her.

" 'Sister, this is Anita Bryant,' I said. Anita always had been one of her favorite people. This tiny little smile came over her face.

"Anita leaned over her and began to sing 'Jesus Loves Me.'

"Now Sister really was in a coma, but those little tears trickled down her face. I just know God really sent Anita to give Sister that message.

"A few days later Sister died. It comforts me to know she was welcomed into the place where she was going, through Jesus sending her that precious little song.

"And Bob, I love that story, because it's so indicative of the way Anita allows herself to be open to the Lord for His use of her."

Teddy, I believe that. And this is what it's all about. Anita provides a good witness to me, for one, and I'm asking the Lord to give me her kind of joy and boldness.

I'm believing for it. After all, Jesus said, "Ask, and ye shall receive."

10 Love and Friction

Despite what Bob just wrote, I do make mistakes in witnessing. Big mistakes, sometimes. The hurt that developed between Charlotte Topping and me—Charlotte, my special sister in Christ!—is a case in point.

Leading Charlotte to Christ had been one of the biggest thrills of my life. Her commitment to Jesus ultimately influenced every other member of her family to give his life to the Lord. This miracle permeated the pages of my book *Amazing Grace*.

Now Charlotte announced her decision to return to her own denomination. We were all at a morning prayer group, just sharing, and this news hit me like a bombshell. I thought she was making a terrible mistake, and I really argued with her.

"You didn't save me, after all, Anita," Charlotte said at one point. "God did."

I came home from the meeting feeling sick, and I just

119

bawled. I had invested heavily in the Topping family and loved every one of them—and now it felt like the rug was being pulled out.

I felt I had to defend our church—not because Northwest Baptist or any other church necessarily represents *the* faith—but here was where she got saved—where she found the Lord.

Also, I knew that was where I get nourished, and I did feel instrumental in leading her to the Lord. So I protested to Charlotte—*very* vocally.

At that point I was quite zealous and dogmatic. Instead of seeing that Charlotte's decision—right or wrong—could be used of the Lord, I felt overly concerned, like it almost was a tragedy.

Marabel, to my surprise, sided with Charlotte. I got so mad at her that we didn't speak for a whole weekend.

I had to get some perspective on this thing before I could realize I had given Charlotte everything I had to give, but there comes a time where you step back and let the Holy Spirit take over.

You quit babying the new believer. You let him stand on his own two feet.

But at that time it hurt me, because I sincerely loved her and thought she was doing a bad thing. I didn't want her to return to a church which might not give her a good foundation in the Bible. (At least, so I reasoned. *After all,* I thought, *she had not been into the Bible at all until she started attending Northwest Baptist. How did I know she would continue the habit?*)

"What if God wants me to take what I've found, and become a firebrand in my own congregation?" Charlotte asked. Marabel sided with her.

"But Charlotte, how can you do that if you're not even grounded in the Word?" I asked. "Maybe that's what God wants you to do eventually, but you can't be impatient. You have to let God take you through the learning process."

After that, there was a coolness between us. It was to be a long while before Charlotte and I could return to where we had been together. I took the whole thing personally—which was wrong—and felt quite put down and disappointed.

Yet I guess she had to say what she did in order to make a clean break. And in fairness, her children did want to return to the church they knew. I understood that.

So I talked to Brother Bill and told him how I felt. I asked him to pray for us. He helped me overcome my wounded feelings and begin to get the whole thing in perspective.

"If this change is God's will for her life, praise the Lord," he said. "We don't know. We must wait and see."

All this time, of course, God was arranging a healing for us. Marabel and I patched things up after a cool and stormy weekend.

"I used to think you were like the Apostle Paul," I told her, "but now I know you're like me. You're Peter." I really was put out with Marabel!

Marabel just continued in her sweet, quiet, loving way to understand and pray for both of us. Meanwhile, as weeks passed, I swore to myself that I'd never again mention the church or anything like that to Charlotte. I could see this bothered her, but I remained stubborn.

She eventually let me know, by casual references, that she was back in her congregation. But I didn't mention churchgoing, Brother Bill, or anything. Nevertheless, slowly but surely, we became able to speak, in general terms, of the Lord.

You cannot love someone and still hold a grudge. And no matter how right you think you are, love is more important

than being right. The raw places steadily began to heal over.
The Lord was working.

Then Charlotte, Marabel, and I went to a spa for a week
for my birthday present. I prayed the three of us would get
back into full fellowship.

The Lord always hears that kind of prayer. That week
not only was physically refreshing—which we all needed—
but it was so sweet in every way. Marabel and I had agreed
that this would be a spiritual renewal. It also turned out to
be so much fun. Each night we prayed together. Charlotte
prayed silently and Marabel and I prayed out loud. And
we all shared, in deep, tender ways, how the Holy Spirit of
God is leading in our lives.

Eventually Charlotte's church had a Faith Alive weekend.
There was an altar call at her church that Sunday, and
Charlotte led the others to the altar. Three of her children
followed her. She said nearly everyone in her church surged
forward toward the altar—this in a church which ordinarily
doesn't have altar calls—and they had a revival!

"God wanted me to return for this," she told me.

She also shared how one of her young sons testified,
"Anita Bryant led our family to the Lord."

I still wish Charlotte had stayed within a church I felt
would really nourish a new Christian—Northwest Baptist,
of course. But I have come to see that this is a transaction
which should be between Charlotte Topping and the Lord.
And if I believe the Holy Spirit guides her life, I must not
be jealous of what happens within it.

Here's another case for letting go and letting God! And
again, for claiming Romans 8:28!

Recently I gave a surprise luncheon for Charlotte's birthday. I made very elaborate preparations and it really was

a surprise. In fact, she was shocked. She showed up wearing an old cotton shirt, her hair pulled back and no makeup—and I *knew* she didn't suspect.

It was really wonderful. All the friends, the presents, and fun, and everything—and it turned into a time of sharing, because so many of those girls had trusted the Lord and the others were searching.

I tell this story because obviously it has taught me some important lessons.

Most important, I am learning that being right is not paramount with Christians. Acting loving is the main thing. As it says in 1 John 4:7, "Beloved, let us love one another: for love is of God; and every one that loveth is born of God, and knoweth God."

Praise the Lord that Charlotte, Marabel, and I—Christian sisters all—do love the Lord and do love one another—even when we disagree!

Anita

11 Small Group Dynamics

Some of the most amazing Christian growth I ever saw came
about through the small-group concept Teddy Heard initi-
ated in our summer camp.

I promised to share some of these techniques with you,
because this concept can be used in classrooms, dormito-
ries, sororities and fraternities, athletic teams and anywhere
else that sharing in a deeply honest and personal way is
important.

Teddy Heard is writing a book about what she has
learned through small-group experiences. Some of our camp
adventures will be included. Meanwhile, though, let's see
exactly what the Holy Spirit helped her establish at Bibletown—that open, exciting climate which helped free so
many little girls from their own self-doubts and shyness.

Our camp sessions lasted only a week. It was important
to find a way to help the girls get acquainted with one

another right away, to start building new relationships in trust and confidence. That's a pretty tall order.

Teddy aimed toward three areas of development within the girls' experience: Personal Growth, Group Building (an opportunity for them to experience communion with one another), and Mission, which sent them out even beyond their group. Each group session included exercises in these three areas.

The girls learned that they were going to experience in just one week how it feels to love someone and be loved. They could apply this experience to their futures again and again—especially in school, we told them, with new friends.

Here's how we operated. We had each counselor sit down with her group of about eight girls. During the first session we tried to make them aware of one another and direct their attention away from themselves, so they wouldn't feel homesick, embarrassed, or self-conscious.

Teddy helped the counselors find good ways to go around the circle, giving each girl a chance to know something about the others. They asked very simple questions: What is your name? How many brothers and sisters do you have? What is your favorite thing to do, and what do you do best?

These questions opened them up to one another. Right away each girl gained seven new friends and knew some fundamental things about each one.

The questions continued. How did you hear about the camp, and what sounded most interesting about it? What was your warmest relationship between ages seven and twelve? What does it mean to you to be a good friend?

The first day, Teddy gave the girls a dramatić assignment.

"Make a new friend today," she told them. "Your ticket to supper tonight will be your new friend.

"This afternoon your counselors will remind you to find your new friend, but we will not help you do this. You can sit with your new friend at supper and find out one thing about her that you can share with the rest of us."

That evening at supper Teddy took the microphone and interviewed some of the girls. "Did you ask her to be your friend, or did she ask you?" she asked.

"I asked her."

"How did you feel before you asked?"

"Oh, I was embarrassed."

"Why did you choose this girl for a friend?"

"She looked like she would say yes."

"Isn't it wonderful that we can be a person who looks like we'll respond if someone wants to be our friend?"

It was fun talking over the microphone. Everyone laughed and loosened up. At last Teddy asked, "What did this show you about how people feel when they don't know anybody?"

"This showed me that everybody wants somebody to come be their friend," one girl said. Even the adults came out of that session with a totally new feeling about giving love and initiating friendship. Really, we're all hungry for it.

Once again we realize what Jesus knows—that we all need to be loved, and we need to love. If we can show our own personality and who we are, we're usually going to be accepted.

The next morning, Teddy passed out pencils and paper and asked the girls four questions:

Do you think it's easy or hard to make a new friend?
What part is hard for you?
In what way did this experience help you know how to make friends at school next fall? And what goals would you set for yourself in being a friend?

You would be amazed at some of the very honest and analytical answers these questions provoked. It was very exciting.

At another group session, Teddy helped the girls analyze their own feelings. They asked themselves what qualities are apparent in the kind of individuals they were able to establish deep and intimate relationships with. Teddy asked them to think of some person with whom they had a meaningful relationship, and to do some analytical work on it.

That meeting lasted three hours. They enjoyed it so much —they became totally absorbed.

By the way, this was the group of questions Teddy tried out on the group of gals who met at my house before the camp opened—adults. They all considered it a rare opportunity to sit down and have that kind of fellowship, where you expressed the way you really felt, what turns you on, and what turns you off in a relationship.

Jody Dunton, during this session, felt she gained a whole new insight into the kind of person God wanted her to be to other people. About an hour later, Teddy received a phone call from one woman who had been present.

She had gone home in the car with another mother with whom she had had a problem of very poor communication for a year. It had gotten so bad it really was a stumbling block to both families.

"If we could sit there and be that honest and talk that openly this morning, I feel like I want to be honest with you," one girl said. "I want to tell you I've had a very difficult time expressing myself to you."

"Have I done anything to create this gap?" the other girl asked.

So they talked the whole thing out for the first time, and

prayed and cried together. The one who phoned Teddy was in tears as she told the story.

Teddy said this shows again what happens when *we* don't try to dominate or force changes, but sit together as the body of Christ, and allow His Spirit to move in the lives of people. Things can happen through the resources of ten people that never could happen if just one person stands up in front of a group and gives a lesson about something.

I asked Teddy to give some pointers about how the small groups operated so successfully with young girls the age of ours. This comes directly from her unedited taped answer.

"First, we had to enable the little girls to feel perfectly safe.

"That could be done in various ways: for example, not speaking out of strength but out of weakness. In other words, if someone comes up with a problem, don't give the answer, but go back into yourself and say, 'When did I have a problem like that?'

" 'What was the problem, and how did I learn the answer?'

"The moment we give the right answer, the glib answer, it cuts everybody off.

"Another thing is, do not ever say you *should* do something, or you *ought* to do something. Instead, explain in a loving way that such and such is a very good thing to know. The group leader should try never to be an advice-giver.

"Leading groups, in my opinion, implies the opposite of teaching. You want to 'become as a little child,' so you can identify with the little girls, or the weak or troubled adult.

"The idea is to love and accept them where they are, not to try to make them think we are trying to change them to become what we want them to be. The purpose of the group is not to solve problems, but to serve as an outlet for individuals to learn to express how they feel.

"Therefore, have a rule that you use only what you have learned out of your own life.

"That eliminates all the pet theories you may have gathered together, and leaves only results.

"We taught our little girls that we were interested in what their experiences were. Most children had not had adults really focus at an interest level like that.

"If it were something that wasn't good, or didn't sound good, the leader should say, 'I know how you feel.' The way to make someone feel safe is through using such statements as, 'I know how you feel,' and avoiding such statements as 'You should not feel that way.'

" 'If you could change one thing about your looks, what would it be?' I asked them. The girls discovered that everybody in the circle had lots of things they'd like changed, and it was hard to decide what they wanted changed most.

" 'Anybody who looks at me can tell what I would like to change. My nose is so big!' one girl said.

" 'Oh no, you don't have a big nose,' my reaction might have been.

"But if I had said that she could not have trusted me or believed I understood her. When someone makes a negative statement about himself, my duty as a leader is to try to identify with him in his feelings about himself. All of us can identify that way. I certainly could share my own experience of weakness—which was crooked teeth.

" 'I know how you feel about your big nose, because when I was your age I had very crooked teeth and had to wear braces,' I told her. 'I thought my teeth would always be crooked, and that's why they bothered me.

" 'But when I went to that dentist and he put braces on and showed me how my teeth were going to look after two years of wearing those braces, it became okay to wear the braces and I didn't worry too much any more about my crooked teeth.

" 'Tell me about my teeth now,' I suggested.

" 'They're straight,' she said.

" 'That's right. And did you know that your nose is the first thing that grows on your face? Then your face grows up to your nose. When you get older you won't notice your nose as much as you do now, just as I don't notice my teeth.' "

The Holy Spirit has given Teddy a great ministry through her small-group approach. She always opens with prayer, and asks the Holy Spirit to come and control every word spoken and every responding thought.

In our groups we had a lot to say about prayer. As things came up, Teddy taught the girls to stop and pray about them—a marvelous habit for any of us to learn.

She taught me so very much. It was hard to absorb it all —our experiences were so rich.

"One of the problems about trying to reach other people's deep feelings is, we're not in touch with our own deep feelings," Teddy said. "We tend to cushion ourselves against them, and we don't know what to do about them.

"We have to work through these, or else we won't have a testimony."

12 "Go Ye Into All the World"

We always like to get new members in our church, but the sad thing is, we're getting new members from churches which are not fulfilling their members' spiritual needs.

So many churches today preach a namby-pamby social gospel—and that's because this whole country operates on a principle of supply and demand.

People talk about pornography and obscenity in the movies and on television, the radio and the newsstands—but still, this is a commercial country, and it's supply and demand.

People wouldn't be making these X-rated movies and printing these magazines if there were not a demand for them. If things were reversed and people wanted more Christian books, movies, and TV shows, that's what they'd make.

I think preachers and churches fall victim to these same principles.

Preachers probably go into a new church with their hearts set on really preaching the gospel but they wear down, and end up preaching the sermons their people want to hear.

Most male churchgoers don't want to come on a Sunday morning and be put under conviction. The ladies in their nice hats don't want to be told they are sinners. As a result, many preachers give sermons the people want to hear.

Can the individual Christian really make much of an impact on this highly secular world? How do we fight moral pollution? Is there any use to try?

If you have children, what I'm about to relate may shock you. I hope so.

Recently I was talking to Senator Mark Hatfield of Oregon, a Christian friend of ours. We had come to Washington, D.C., on business and right off I ran smack into a hassle with one of our government agencies—the Federal Communications Commission, better known as the FCC.

"Mark, I'm into a thing with the FCC about radio stations, particularly the acid rock FM stations which broadcast obscene materials," I told him.

"I'm getting nowhere. The thing is, very few parents realize their kids are buying records and albums and listening to stations that are broadcasting obscene material. The parents don't know it's obscene."

"Don't *know?*" someone asked me.

It's a big problem. Do parents go out and do research on the kind of lingo the kids are into these days?

Do they go out and study a course on obscene words and all that?

When I explain to some parents the double meanings and what the true meanings of some of these hit records are, they're flabbergasted. The generations change and slang changes, but of course I keep up with pop music, and for that reason am becoming increasingly disturbed by what I hear.

You listen to lyrics today and when they say something like "I'm floating in a dream world," they mean high on drugs. Parents have to be aware of what their kids are reading and listening to these days.

When people intend to see an X-rated movie they have to pay for it, buy a ticket, and make a move to go in. But we were driving home one night, and I accidentally tuned in to an FM station. (In broadcasting, there's a factor called accidental dialing, and you and your children can fall victim to it.) We punched up this radio station that was broadcasting obscene material. Out-and-out *obscene*.

They played a record album, then gave commercials for obscene movies, complete with dirty language. Since the airwaves belong to the public, theoretically no station is allowed to do that.

As a former disc jockey, I knew exactly what to do about the situation—or so I thought. I wrote a letter to the Federal Communications Commission and gave every imaginable detail: time, title of the album, station call letters—everything.

I received a form letter in reply!

When we later went to Washington, I made a point of telephoning the FCC to register my complaint again. I simply couldn't understand why my letter didn't rate a real reply. The thing that bugged me was that the form letter said, "What you may consider obscene—words like *damn* and *hell*—we can't do anything about, because we don't consider these obscene."

But I had been much more specific than that. I had repeated the exact words, and there's *no way* anyone would not consider them filthy. To my surprise, the FCC spokesman said I'd probably have problems in pursuing this thing further—because nobody ever has!

I was really amazed at that.

Here we are in the United States of America, supposedly a Christian country, and nobody is attacking this problem. Here we are, a majority of people supposedly against obscene material, yet we can't seem to gather enough strength to make some noise in Washington!

"I really think there are Christians living in towns across America who really are not aware that this filth is on the air," I told Mark Hatfield at dinner that night. He and Antoinette said the same situation exists just outside Washington.

What can we do about it?

I wish parents would find out what stations their kids listen to, then just take an afternoon or evening some time and monitor them. Find out exactly what their kids are hearing. Find out exactly what's on the air.

Now I'm not advocating censorship. I'm saying some record companies take responsibility for the decency of their records—but a lot do not. As a parent, you're doubtless vitally interested in what goes into your child's head—and some of our kids listen to this stuff hours each day.

This could undermine our country. You don't have to win wars on the battlefield any more. You can win wars by winning the minds of men, and destroying a country from within—by broadcasting garbage over the radio, for example.

The reason this problem is so tricky is, you could play the top forty tunes to any senator or congressman today and he probably couldn't translate the little innuendoes in the lyrics. Most adults don't know what's going on!

Some records produced these days are fine, played at air speed, but the kids know you can play the record at another speed and the obscenities come out—so these records sell millions of copies.

The FCC monitors commercials and monitors programs very conscientiously. But what they don't do is screen all current records and albums for possible adverse meanings. Therefore, we parents need to do it.

I suggest you note all details. Get specifics. Tape portions of these obscene broadcasts, if necessary. From my own experience I'd say you'll probably only get a form letter if you complain to the FCC, but we definitely ought to inform our congressmen. Remember, however, they have to have very complete details—date, time, station, program—and, unfortunately, it has to consist of raw, obvious obscenities, in an obscene context.

Meanwhile, we Christians sit back complacently and let the devil work. We're not coming out even in the battle. The devil too often controls the airwaves our children listen to.

At the same time, you and I, out witnessing for Jesus, have only so wide a sphere of influence. You take one radio station that at any given moment has thousands of kids listening to it—and they've got a lot of power there.

How many people can you reach, in comparison to the lewd radio program, the cheap TV program, that reaches thousands or even millions?

I'm saying the Christian has a duty to object to all this garbage, but first he has to find out where it is. To what radio station does my child listen? What music does it broadcast? What are the words of the records my child listens to? What are they buying? What do these words mean? And if a child listens to a couple of hours of this garbage a day, is that offset by a couple of hours of wholesome Christian activity? How about Bible reading?

If a child goes to church one hour a week, that will in no way counterbalance the bad influence he gets just from the radio, much less all the non-Christian influences he is exposed to at school, the movies, magazines, and everywhere else, and the kid is just snowed under.

These rules, of course, apply to adults, also. The devil is in there working.

Jesus said, "Go ye into all the world and preach the gospel . . ." (Mark 16:15).

How far do we go?

How far do we permit un-Christian influences to go?

And when will we sing, with the Psalmist David:

Let the words of my mouth, and the meditation of my heart, be acceptable in thy sight, O Lord, my strength, and my redeemer.   Psalms 19:14

13 "One Nation Under God"

When Anita sings "God Bless America" it makes people weep.

She sings it as a prayer. She really means it like a prayer, and they give her a standing ovation. Nobody can hear "God Bless America" and not say to himself, deep in his heart, "Amen."

America is still one nation under God. And no matter how we criticize our country—and we all do, if we love her—and no matter how much the world criticizes us, we still know we are God's people.

The Bible says, in Psalms 33:12, "Blessed is the nation whose God is the Lord; and the people whom he hath chosen for his own inheritance."

Anita and I have been privileged to meet many of these "chosen people"—true patriots, both famous and unknown.

The Lord has blessed us with some super-heavy experiences. In all kinds of impressive circumstances, we have been thrown together with presidents, statesmen, religious and in-

dustrial leaders, and military heroes. It's the kind of thing
that makes you believe in America.

These days, however, it's become pretty popular to knock
our country and talk about how rotten it's getting. This is
very bad.

America as a nation has a witness. It's still a fact that God
has sustained our country through everything in our history.

God is alive in America today. He lives in Bible-believing
churches, in Christ-centered homes, and in Spirit-filled people
who are willing to witness for Jesus.

It might be easy enough to lose sight of this fact. But there
comes a time—like the day President Lyndon Baines Johnson
was buried—that the greatness of the United States of America floods over your soul.

President Johnson had expressed a desire for Anita to "sing
when I'm lowered into the ground." He had wanted Billy
Graham, the evangelist, to preach at his burial.

The world watched that day as we buried a great president.
It made a really great, unique kind of national witness for
the Lord. It's something Anita and I will never forget.

*Bob and I happened to be in Austin, Texas, for an impor-
tant booking the day President Johnson died. It was late
afternoon. We had finished rehearsing and I was taking a
bath. Bob came into the room.*

"Anita, I have some bad news. President Johnson died."

"Oh no, Bob! No!"

*I reacted with shock, with the kind of dismay you feel
when it's your own family. I really related to him. He was
big and warm and outgoing, and as natural and homespun
in his attitudes as my own father is.*

My mind flew all over the place. We had invited the

Johnsons to hear our show that night, but we'd learned the president wasn't physically able to attend. Pat and Luci Nugent, son-in-law and daughter of the president, were coming instead. We planned to settle on a time when our family would visit the Johnsons at the LBJ ranch—an invitation they had several times extended.

Should I do the show? What kind of cloud would be over the evening? I felt great sadness and confusion. This was such a gigantic, dynamic man. He had been so real to me.

When you had known him not just as a president, but as a father image, and when you had seen him as a fond grandfather, and had touched his life in a way that he responded to you with a real love . . . .

Immediately I realized I had not prayed for this family's needs. I went into the bedroom of our hotel and prayed for the Lord to minister to them, to keep them strong, to provide comfort. I knew the next days would be really tough. And I also prayed for myself, that I would display Christian courage during the show that night.

After the prayer, I tried to reach Luci Johnson Nugent by telephone. I wanted her to know we were praying for her. She was on her way to the ranch, of course, and impossible to reach, but a friend promised to relay my message.

And then we did the show. We played a convention of Texas Oil Jobbers that night, and there were many friends of Lyndon B. Johnson in the audience. During the show I decided to address myself to the topic that was on everyone's mind.

"Today we all lost a great president and a friend," I told them. "For my friend Lyndon Baines Johnson—this song is for him."

The song was "Battle Hymn of the Republic," of course.

I had sung it for him a number of times before, in the White House and elsewhere, and he never failed to come to his feet.

Now I had to pray for the strength to sing it and not break up. Somehow I did it, to my surprise, but it was hard that night to sing anything at all, in that room where his friends wept for him.

Back at the hotel, we went right to bed. I lay there in the dark, remembering. Just two months before, we had filled an engagement in Austin during the time Luci had been hospitalized with a painful ear operation.

Marabel Morgan, Teddy Heard, and I went to the hospital to visit Luci. She really was too ill to receive visitors, but they let me slip into her room for a moment. The President was stretched out on a lounge chair in her room.

He had seemed happy to see me. I just took his hand and talked to him, noting that he looked really drawn and tired. "We've got to get you to the ranch," he kept saying. "I want you to bring the whole family," he insisted. "But make it soon. Don't put it off now."

Then he said he felt quite tired, and wouldn't even try to make it to my performance that evening. "I understand perfectly," I told him. "I wouldn't expect you even to try, with Luci so sick.

"Anyhow, it's the same old act. You've heard it so many times already—the same old 'Battle Hymn of the Republic.'"

"Are you going to sing that?" he asked. Suddenly he looked really wistful. "I'd like to hear it," he told me.

We had a time problem that evening. By the time we visited Luci and then popped in on Teddy Heard's aunt, we had very little time before my show began. What's more, I had become hoarse. Marabel and Teddy prayed for me that the Lord would give me a clear-as-a-bell voice.

Suddenly, at the show site, President Johnson's Secret Service man appeared. "They're coming after all, and bringing a dozen people with them," he told me.

You can imagine how flabbergasted I felt. Before I sang, I acknowledged the Johnsons and their party. From a full heart I said history would record that President Johnson was one of the greatest leaders in our country's history. And of course I said I loved them, and was so touched to see them there, because he was tired and I didn't expect them.

The Lord really was present that night. It was Him singing. He spoke out in my testimony and everything else. And when I sang, He gave me the voice I needed to do "Power and Glory," "God Bless America," and "Battle Hymn of the Republic"—all very demanding numbers.

God anointed the performance. I simply didn't have the voice beforehand, and was quite tired besides—and yet, through the power of God's Holy Spirit, somehow found myself humbled by a standing ovation.

President Johnson, instead of slipping out after the show, came marching up backstage and giving me one of his old bear hugs. He was as glowing as if he had just come in from a Florida vacation. He looked renewed and rejuvenated. I had never seen such a transformation.

The President said my performance brought back the White House days, when I lifted him with my singing. It really turned into such a sweet, exciting evening. He acted just like a youngster.

After they left we stayed for an hour or so, signing autographs and so on, and then the Secret Service man reappeared. President Johnson had sent me his newest photo, taken at the ranch, all signed and everything. He wrote such a sweet inscription:

To Anita and Bob with my appreciation and my love.
Lyndon B. Johnson
LBJ Ranch, Stonewall, Texas, 11/19/72

Luci Nugent returned Anita's phone call at three o'clock
the next morning. When I got Anita to the phone she still
sounded a little groggy with sleep.

"I just wanted you to know we are praying for you," Anita
told Luci. "I didn't expect you to return my call. I knew you
were with family . . . ."

"You know, you *are* family," said Pat Nugent, who was on
an extension phone with Luci.

"Anita, there were so many times you gave pleasure to
Daddy," Luci said. "He thought so much of you and Bob.
Not only did he love your singing—you thrilled him so many
times—but he loved your life, and your Christian witness.
He thought so much of that, and bragged on it.

"Many times he discussed with us, since he loved you both
so much, that when he was buried he wanted you to sing
the 'Battle Hymn of the Republic.' Several times he requested
that."

At that point Anita began to weep. Luci continued to talk,
but as Anita cried, she began to break also. Anita realized
she just couldn't do that to Luci. She brought herself under
control.

I knew she felt overwhelmed to learn that President Johnson had discussed such a thing. She felt highly honored, not
just because he was a president, but to learn that he returned
some of the respect and love she felt for him. I don't blame
her for getting emotional!

Pat Nugent and I tried to work out arrangements. I knew
it would be rough. We had a concert scheduled for that

Thursday night in Tallahassee, Florida, an event the Junior Women's Club there had worked on for months.

The schedule looked impossible. I had a somewhat-sinking feeling as I tried to figure how it could be altered to include this important commitment.

"Trust the Lord that He will work it out," Anita said.

That was good advice. It was absolutely all we could do.

Transportation became the big problem. We worked it out that we could get to Texas okay, but how to make it from there to the concert? Everything was cut too fine—I was feeling uneasy about it and so was Anita. We asked God to send us an answer.

The answer came the next morning via phone call from the White House. A transportation officer said, "Miss Bryant, the President is sending a plane to Miami to take Mr. Bebe Rebozo directly to the LBJ ranch.

"Would you object to riding on that flight to the ranch? Would that help you with your transportation? If so, we could fly you immediately afterwards to Tallahassee to get you to your concert.

"Would that be agreeable?"

Anita said, "Would that be agreeable? You're an answer to prayer!" He laughed.

It turned out that there would be plenty of room on the plane and that we could take Bobby and Gloria with us, if we wished. We decided to pray about it so the Lord could make us confident of the answer.

Both kids had met President Johnson and remembered him well. They had visited him in the White House, where he took quite a bit of time with them and gave them nice gifts. We felt this occasion would be a significant one for them, and I wanted them to be there.

Before the day was over, everything worked out perfectly.

The schools were cooperative, and the kids had no tests scheduled. We decided to take them with us.

As any woman would do, I headed for my clothes closet. All my dresses were bright-colored and inappropriate. I prayed about it, then phoned Charlotte Topping.

"I know you have a slew of black dresses, Charlotte. Bring them out," I told her.

"Don't worry," she comforted me. "If we don't find anything in the closet, I'll take you shopping."

Trouble is, there was no time for shopping. Usually it takes me a whole day to find one thing. And I never, never find shoes with out a big search. My feet are very hard to fit. I prayed about it and asked God to lead us.

This was an important occasion and I wanted to look just right. Charlotte didn't have a suitable dress so we went shopping. Imagine my elation when we found the perfect dress, one I knew was just right—black, with a pale turquoise collar. Definitely it was the dress.

"Charlotte, the dress is perfect. But where will we find some shoes?" I was beginning to feel panicky.

"We've got to trust the Lord for them," Charlotte said, as she led me across the street to a shoe store.

It would take a lot of trust, because the dress needed just the right shoes—and I had nothing appropriate at home. The first pair the man brought out proved to be perfect in every way, including fit, and I walked out saying, "I can't believe it, I can't believe it, I can't believe it!"

"Oh, ye of little faith!" Charlotte said.

Once again I realized how God wants you to turn over to Him the little details of your life. In just an hour, we had done it all!

Back home, Bob had been telephoning, night and day, all

week long. It was a constant round of inquiries, altered plans, cancelled reservations, a million details. Bless his heart, he stayed so patient and cool.

And then we were off! Charlotte Topping had promised to pray for me. As Bob drove toward the airport, I dialed Brother Bill Chapman on our automobile telephone.

I already had phoned Marabel Morgan and begged for their prayers. I thought about phoning Teddy, but instinctively knew there was no need—that she was perfectly attuned to the situation. I knew Gloria Roe would pray, and certain other friends.

But now I phoned Brother Bill—because I just needed him.

"Why are you doing that?" Bob scolded a little. "You're always calling him. Quit bugging him," Bob said.

"Bob, it's his birthday. I want to wish him a happy birthday." So we called, and all of us sang "Happy Birthday" to him. Peggy, his wife, told us later that it touched him.

"Please be sure and pray," I asked him.

"Don't worry," he said. "The Lord is with you, Anita. I'm going to hold you up in my prayers, and you just sing for Jesus."

"I will," I promised, my voice quivering.

One thing sure, I'd have to sing without accompaniment. I tell you, we really prayed about that! All along, Bob said, "No accompaniment."

"I can't do it," I told him.

"It's the only thing you can do," he told me. "Anything else will be inapropos."

"I agree with you there," I admitted, "but this service is being held outside. I've got the elements to contend with. I've only done 'Battle Hymn' a cappella once before in my life—and that was impromptu."

Of course I knew I could sing a cappella. That would not

*be the problem. But the strain and stress, the physical strain,
would not make it easy to sound vocally good.*

*Doubt crept in. I really wasn't terribly sure. But as the days
flew by there seemed to be no alternative. Our orchestra and
conductor had to remain in Tallahassee for our scheduled
concert. Piano accompaniment wouldn't be right for this
occasion, nor did organ or harp seem right.*

Meanwhile, God was working things out.

Anita still had doubts, even as we landed at Bergstrom Air
Force Base in Austin, Texas, where we were to meet the
white and silver *Air Force One* presidential plane which was
bringing the Johnson family, with the body of President
Johnson, from Washington, D.C. There we would join the
procession behind Mrs. Johnson and her daughters, for a
sixty-five mile drive to the burial site.

Texas weather was nasty that day—cold and rainy and
bitter. Friends of the late president arrived: Billy and Ruth
Graham, John and Nellie Connally, members of the Taylor
and Johnson families.

We lined up and waited to greet the presidential plane.
People held umbrellas over us. Soon the Johnson family de-
planed. The coffin, borne by representatives from each of
the armed services, was carried off the rear of the plane. A
band struck up "Ruffles and Flourishes."

As we slowly proceeded to the small burial grounds on the
famous LBJ Ranch, I felt really thankful that I had insisted
Anita sing *a cappella*. I knew we'd go directly into the services. There would have been no rehearsal time possible. As
we rode along in a limousine with Pat Nugent and little Lyn,
and with Brigadier General James U. Cross, President Johnson's former military aide and expilot of *Air Force One,* I said
a little prayer of thanks.

The Lord had sent me the word—okay. From the beginning, I figured best to keep things simple.

"You know you can do it," I told her. "For most other singers it would not be possible, but you can sing *a cappella*. You know when you get up there and sing completely on your own, you know what you can do. Even under the worst circumstances, with a microphone and otherwise on your own, you can do it.

"Anita, if you begin to add unknown factors to this situation—like an orchestra that's unrehearsed, that you can't hear, that may come in incorrectly at certain places—that's when things go completely haywire."

Bob was completely right, as it turned out. There was no chance to warm up vocally, even. What could I do? I just said, as we rode toward the services, "All right, Lord. Start warming up!"

We arrived. It was muddy, and bitter cold. I followed John Connally, who was scheduled to give a few remarks. They sat me near John, and near Billy Graham.

Sitting there was the difficult part. They had placed President Johnson's casket beneath a huge, gnarled oak tree. His family sat close by, and those of us participating in the service. Some ten thousand friends and neighbors thronged the area. Amplifiers carried messages from John Connally and Billy Graham even across the Pedernales River.

Panic began to set in, despite my best efforts. My feet got wet and began to freeze. I had on my fur coat. Always, always I take off my coat before I perform. There's a freedom I need—I can't have anything on my shoulders.

In Korea on one of the Bob Hope Christmas tours I sang with snowflakes big as your fist hitting me in the face, and

I wore a chiffon dress. But we did that for the guys. We gals wanted to do it.

This time, as I sat there, the devil was saying, in my mind, "Better keep your coat on or you'll freeze to death. You're going to shake and lose control of your voice. Keep your coat on!" Even with my coat on, I felt freezing cold.

Then sheer fear began to creep from my toenails up to my head. What if I started to cry?

What if the note that comes out of my mouth is too high? Where do I go from there?

All these panic thoughts flashed through my mind. Then I stuck my hand in my right coat pocket, where I had some insurance (and this shows you the nature of man, how we cling to our security measures!) I had stuck a little pitch pipe in there. And it was cold as ice!

During a prayer I sneaked the pitch pipe out of my pocket and breathed into it softly, desperately trying to hit an A-flat—but no sound emerged. I raised it to my mouth as if I were stifling a cough with my hand, but at that moment the prayer ended. I stuck it back in my pocket real fast.

Cold sweat broke out on me. "All right, Lord. All I can do is trust in You," I said. "Give me an A-flat!"

Immediately the Lord seemed to say, in my mind, "All right, but I expect you to take off your coat. You have on your fishhook pin. If you don't take off your coat, you're hiding the gospel."

That came to me as clearly as if I were hearing Brother Bill preaching to me from the pulpit. I said, "I will, Lord." Instantly the confidence flooded back.

And then I was standing up to sing, totally serene. John Connally set down the footstool which placed me at the right height for the podium. Billy gave me the nod, so I'd

*know when to go up there. Beforehand, I had asked him to
pray for me.*

"Don't worry, I will. But you pray for me," he directed.

*I took off my coat and stood at the podium—and I tell
you, I felt hot! It was as if I had walked into a warm room.
The Presence of the Holy Spirit occupied me.*

*I sang—I don't know whether or not it was an A-flat—
but it was another voice. It was as though I had been waiting up all my life, for that moment.*

*God was in command. It was so quiet there I could hear
the wind rustling the dry leaves as I sang. It was peaceful
there, the Lord's peace, and I felt it.*

*To really sing to Jesus—I remembered what Brother Bill
had said.*

*I kept my eyes closed. When I opened them one time I
saw the casket directly in front of me, so I closed my eyes
again. I had to concentrate on the singing. There were three
key changes, and I had to pay strict attention. I wanted to
sing it exactly as President Johnson had heard it so many
times—the way I thought he'd want me to sing it.*

Anita did exactly what the Lord wanted her to do that
day. Bobby, Gloria, and I were praying for her, of course.
Back home, and elsewhere, we had the comfort of knowing
there were like believers who held her up in prayer.

It was an awesome responsibility, the most difficult thing
she had ever done, but I think she had a confidence that
showed—a strength from the Lord.

You'd have to imagine the situation—an emotional occasion, for one thing—the funeral of a man she cared for quite
a lot. The weather was most unideal for singing, of course—

the raw, wet cold, the wind. And there was no accompaniment whatever.

But I had a confidence for her. Anita in the eyes of other show-business people may not be the world's biggest star, but I cannot think of another star anywhere who has appeared in as many prestigious and pressure situations as Anita has—the Orange Bowl, the Super Bowl, the Royal Palace in Bangkok, the White House—oh, too many to mention! And always, singing difficult things.

Also, I reflected that she can bare her soul in public—like in the Billy Graham Crusades. That's the ultimate in pressure for someone, that you can confess your sins publicly.

Add to that adverse conditions—the Bob Hope trips, snow, heat, rain, everything. Add to that state fairs, county fairs, rodeos, summer stock—things that are really rough to do. She has run the whole entertainment spectrum, and never has insisted on or even expected ideal conditions.

Anita is used to big audiences and rugged conditions. She is versatile and adaptable, and this has to have a cumulative effect on a person's self-confidence.

Suddenly I felt proud of Anita's poise and self-control, proud of the quality of her performance, proud of her Christian faith that produces an indomitable toughness when circumstances call for it.

As Anita sang, I watched the faces of the Johnson women —strong, serene, courageous. Lynda Robb mouthed the words of the hymn as Anita sang it. Lynda's face radiated joy and faith. Mrs. Johnson and Luci Nugent seemed totally absorbed in the message of this tremendous hymn.

John Connally and others said to me afterwards, remarking on the calm and victorious attitudes of the president's family and the beautiful way they involved themselves in the service: "That's the way he would have wanted them to be."

As Anita sang, it came to me that every one of those ten thousand participants in the burial services for the thirty-sixth president of these United States in a way provided a witness for the world.

I thought how this great president, who had come up from humble circumstances, at the last chose to ignore pomp and ceremony. His burial ceremonies were the essence of simplicity.

I thought about Dr. Billy Graham, who had grown up in the hills of North Carolina, and had gone forth to preach the gospel into all the world. I thought how this very ordinary and extraordinary man, Billy Graham, had been used of the Lord throughout this country and the rest of the world—more than any other evangelist who ever lived.

And now he was telling us, "He loved this hill country. President Johnson once said, 'I love this country where people know when you are sick, love you while you are alive, and miss you when you die.'"

And I thought with wonder about Anita Bryant, a young American who grew up around the oil fields of Oklahoma, a girl who gave her life to Christ when she was only eight years old, who went on to grow up and become not only a star—but a wife and mother and a powerful Christian witness.

There was something peculiarly American about these ceremonies, and this day. It was more than the simplicity, touching as that was. Rather, it was your sudden realization that the gathering included the great and the illustrious—represented every political faction—and gathered to that ranch home by the Pedernales River black and white peo-

*ple, young and old, rich and poor, famous and humble—
people who loved an ordinary man who went on to become
great.*

*As my eyes scanned the rows of participants, I felt a sense
of awe to realize how many highly placed Americans in
this gathering also are outstanding Christians. Muriel and
Hubert Humphrey—Representative John W. McCormack,
Speaker of the House—John and Nellie Connally—and
many, many more.*

People made over Anita a lot, afterwards. I believe they
perceived the presence of the Lord in her.

"What a testimony you gave us today!" one man told her.
"Praise the Lord!"

Mrs. Johnson, poised and victorious, turned almost immediately after the ceremony and spoke to Anita. "This is
what Lyndon would have wanted," she said. "It was perfect, and it would have pleased him."

We stopped at the ranch to pay our respects to the President's family. "Come on inside. You all must be tired and
hungry," Lady Bird Johnson said.

You had to admire that strength. She was really tremendous. "I've been praying for you all this time," Anita told
her. "You really are a testimony and a witness to me."

Mrs. Johnson turned a serene and glowing smile on her.
"As I stood in the library the other day, receiving our friends
and neighbors as Lyndon's body lay in state, a young man
came up to me.

"He was dressed in long hair and hippie-type clothing.
He said something very profound to me. He said, 'Be proud.
Smile and be happy. You have so much to be happy for and
proud of.' "

Mrs. Johnson said it really struck home to her that they had had thirty-eight long, wonderful years. That was her attitude, and it was beautiful.

Soon *Air Force One* was rushing us to Tallahassee, Florida, where a great audience had waited more than an hour for Anita to arrive. The concert was fantastic.

Mr. Rebozo came on to the concert with us to hear Anita perform and then to complete our journey home.

Governor Reubin Askew was there. It struck me again, with much force, how fortunate we are to live in a state where the governor is a vigorous and outspoken Christian.

My mind wandered back to Washington, D.C., where we had visited with two of our favorite Christians—Senator and Mrs. Mark Hatfield.

We had enjoyed dinner with Mark and Antoinette, and they were driving us back to our hotel. Suddenly Anita exclaimed, "Oh, we forgot to pray!"

Mark immediately pulled the car over and parked beside a row of distinguished-looking houses. Mark and I were in the front seat, the girls in back. We all held hands—each guy holding one hand of each gal—and looking like a bunch of contortionists!

We prayed aloud, one by one. Later we laughed about what the people in those houses must have thought if they looked out and saw these four people so strangely entwined.

Yes, I thought, this country does have fantastic Christians in high places. We do have strength which comes from the Lord.

Despite scandals, travails, and depressions of the national spirit, America still belongs to God.

Will Americans continue to witness to Him?

Will we train up our children to worship Him?

Will we become obedient to His instructions about carrying the gospel into all the world?

What will our nation's testimony become during the years ahead? If we falter, God will surely judge us as He did Sodom and Gomorrah.

In the long run, this nation or any other can only go back to the Bible. We must do as Joshua commanded:

> Choose you this day whom ye will serve
> . . . as for me and my house, we will serve the Lord.

If American households continue to choose Him, He will continue to bless America.

Praise the Lord!